1967 BENJAMIN F. FAIRLESS MEMORIAL LECTURES

Library of Congress Catalog Card Number 68-24703

# Planning and productivity under Soviet socialism

Abram Bergson

© 1968 CARNEGIE-MELLON UNIVERSITY

Distributed by Columbia University Press
New York-London

The Benjamin F. Fairless Memorial Lectures endowment fund has been established at Carnegie-Mellon University to support an annual series of lectures. An internationally known figure from the worlds of business, government, or education will be invited each year to present three lectures at Carnegie-Mellon under the auspices of its Graduate School of Industrial Administration. In general, the lectures will be concerned with some aspects of business or public administration; the relationships between business and government, management and labor; or a subject related to the themes of preserving economic freedom, human liberty, and the strengthening of individual enterprise — all of which were matters of deep concern to Mr. Fairless throughout his career.

The lecturer will, whenever possible, spend three weeks in residence on the Carnegie-Mellon campus, during which time he will be available for discussions with faculty and students.

---

Mr. Fairless was president of United States Steel Corporation for fifteen years, and chairman of the board from 1952 until his retirement in 1955. A friend of Carnegie Institute of Technology for many years, he served on the board of Trustees from 1952 until his death. In 1959 he was named honorary chairman of the board. He was also a leader and co-chairman of Carnegie Tech's ten-year development program, from its beginning in 1957.

1967

seven

Dr. Abram Bergson, Harvard professor of economics, is director of the University's Russian Research Center, a post he assumed in 1964. He is the author of numerous studies on Russia's economic growth and planning.

Dr. Bergson has taught at the University of Texas and Columbia University, as well as at Harvard. He holds his undergraduate degree from Johns Hopkins University and his graduate degrees from Harvard.

During World War II, he served in the Office of Strategic Services (OSS), with the final title of Chief, Russian Economic Subdivision. Dr. Bergson has been a consultant to the Department of State, Office of Science and Technology, the Arms Control and Disarmament Agency, the RAND Corporation, and various federal agencies.

# Preface

The Benjamin F. Fairless Lectures from which this volume originated were given at Carnegie-Mellon University on November 2, 9, and 16, 1967. I have published the lectures more or less as they were delivered, though I include here some passages in the original text that were omitted orally.

The lectures were prepared for an audience consisting chiefly of invited business executives. It may be hoped, therefore, that this volume will be of interest to non-specialists, but I have felt that it might be more useful generally if I should add documentary and other notes, where these seemed in order. I have also included an Appendix which explains very briefly the derivation of comparative data that are presented on productivity in different countries.

I am much indebted to Professor Simon Kuznets for searching comments on an earlier version, and have also benefited from valuable suggestions by Professor Gottfried Haberler. As the reader of the Appendix will see, in compiling comparative data on productivity I have drawn heavily on Edward F. Denison, *Why Growth Rates Differ*, Washington, D. C., 1967. I am the more obligated to Dr. Denison since he kindly allowed me to refer to his study prior to its publication. My thanks are also due to Miss Mary Towle, for her usual exemplary secretarial aid.

I wish to express my appreciation also to President H. Guyford Stever and his associates at Carnegie-Mellon University for the most kind hospitality that they extended me during my successive visits there.

Abram Bergson

Cambridge, Massachusetts

# I. An attempt at measurement

# I. An attempt at measurement

*Introduction*

This is a very special occasion on which to speak about Russia. It is now fifty years almost to the day since the Bolsheviks initiated the insurrection which first brought them to power in that country. This was certainly a momentous event. It literally shook the world, and has continued ever since to reverberate almost everywhere.

It has also continued to be celebrated, and its semicentennial is now being observed with special ceremony. But the celebrants surely are mainly adherents of the novel ideology that guided the November Revolution to begin with. Among others, the inclination is rather to reflect soberly on the nature and meaning of this event. This one may do with varying emphases and orientation, but a student of economics is impelled to engage in an inquiry of a particular kind. The inquiry, however, may also be of interest to the more general observer.

Against fearful odds, a ruthless party group seized power in a great state, and then somehow retained it. This was an extraordinary feat, but the aim avowedly was to build a radically new kind of society, one superior not only to its predecessor in Tsarist Russia, but to the admittedly more advanced rival type in the West. The new society was to be superior to Western capitalism generally, but particularly in the cardinal economic sphere.

Indeed, in building the novel social system that was projected, the revolutionaries could feel that they were but the instruments of a history already revealed, for the new system, of course, was to be socialism as conceived by Marx. The great analyst of social systems had long ago concluded theoretically that such a society would be economically superior to capitalism. According to the materialist view of history that he also urged, it was but a corollary of such economic superiority that in due time socialism would also come into being. Socialism could even be confidently expected to become pre-eminent.

In the event, socialism has materialized, and not only in Russia. It is now the way of life of over one third of the world's population. Curiously, it has become so in circumstances entirely different from those Marx envisaged. This is a familiar theme that I need not elaborate here. No one needs to be told either that where established, socialism cannot have functioned economically quite as flawlessly as Marx predicted. Clearly capitalism too has hardly evolved in accord with his somber prophecies.

But these are externalities, and from the experience with socialism to date one properly seeks further insight into the issue that Marx in effect posed, that concerning the comparative economic merit of socialism. What in particular of his claim as to the economic superiority of this system over Western capitalism?

Marx's claim has not gone unchallenged even on an abstract plane. Rather it has been subject to continuing attack through the years. And later-day adherents of the Marxian view, for their part, have not been slow to try theoretically to rebut his challengers. The substantial speculative literature that has thus been produced includes writings by many illustrious figures: such as Oskar Lange, among socialists, and Ludwig Mises and Friedrich Hayek, among the critically inclined. Almost inevitably, then, the theoretic exchanges that have occurred are fascinating conceptually. But it is fair to say that they have not been especially conclusive. At least they have not seemed so except perhaps to the more partisan. In trying to judge comparative economic merit, we still have reason to go beyond theoretic speculation to consider the experience with socialism in practice.[1]

A way of economic life admittedly has non-economic effects. No one who values human life, freedom, and dignity will be inclined to appraise the two rival systems solely or even primarily in economic terms. Yet, comparative economic merit is an important issue, and beliefs about it are apt to be consequential. One need not subscribe to Marx's economic determinism to feel that this is so.

Such beliefs are apt to be consequential both for choices between systems, where such choices occur, and for choices among economic institutions within either system. Choices of the latter sort have long been familiar under capitalism. As each day's news reminds us, they seem about to become a habit also under socialism. As a result, the two systems have come to bear only a very partial relation to the alternatives Marx depicted. They are certainly not as dissimilar. But their comparative economic performance is still of interest.

These lectures, let me explain, are devoted to this theme. Concerning the economic functioning of socialism in practice, there have now been published in the West a good many illuminating scholarly writings. Taking these studies as a point of departure, I propose to inquire summarily what may be concluded from the experience with socialism as to the comparative economic merit of this system.

I shall focus particularly on the country where the semicentennial of the November Revolution is now being observed. As the anniversary reminds us, socialism has endured longer in the Soviet Union than it has anywhere else. Socialism thus has had the greatest opportunity to perfect itself in that country. However well or badly socialism may have functioned elsewhere, it should not be at its worst economically in the USSR. Accounts of socialism in other countries only seem to confirm this supposition.

Our knowledge of the economic performance of socialism even in the USSR, however, leaves something to be desired. For socialism elsewhere it is still more limited. This must be considered when we try to generalize from the Soviet experience.

Socialism is understood here as Marx understood it, and as I think it is usually understood: as a system where public ownership of the means of production is predominant. The Soviet Union, however, is also a country where a Communist Party rules. The Party considers itself to be a political heir of Marx.

How pleased Marx would have been at this is an interesting question. But whatever his attitude might have been, we must consider that, in the case of the USSR, socialism is of a politically special sort. Under socialism, however, communist authoritarianism thus far seems to have been rarely if ever avoided in any country, though admittedly the degree has varied.[2] Of course, many proponents of socialism sincerely aspire to avoid authoritarianism of any sort. Some persons regard themselves as socialists who do not seek thoroughgoing public ownership to begin with.

*Normative standards*

What is economic merit? How is it to be gauged? For purposes of normative appraisal of the working arrangements — the institutions, policies, and practices — that determine how a society functions economically, technical writings offer two basic but complementary standards. One is equity, or the degree to which the relative material status of different members of the community approaches some state that is held to be ideal. The other is efficiency. The economist's conception of this standard is rather special, and is not always clearly grasped. Essentially it is seen as of two kinds: static and dynamic.

What a community can accomplish economically at any time, it is understood, depends on the available knowledge of technologies of production and related activities. Such knowledge ultimately delimits the material results achievable with available labor and wealth, and so in effect the economic opportunities that are open. Static efficiency is the degree to which, equity apart, the community is in fact able to exploit the economic opportunities that are open. Alternatively, static efficiency is the degree to which the community succeeds in approaching an economic optimum, where opportunities that are open are fully exploited.

Technological knowledge, however, is not immutable, nor is the effectiveness of its exploitation. At least if the community is at all modern, technological knowledge will normally be continually expanding as a result of new inventions. Such knowledge tends also to be advanced through the borrowing

fifteen

from abroad of technologies already developed there. Moreover, the community may exploit available technological knowledge with varying effect at different times. As the economic optimum shifts with the advance of technological knowledge, so too may the community's approach to it. Dynamic efficiency relates to the community's capacity as time passes to add in one way or another to its technological knowledge and also to improve its exploitation of such knowledge.

Static efficiency, then, refers to performance in utilizing technological possibilities existing at one time; dynamic efficiency, to capacity for self-improvement through enlargement of technological possibilities and their more effective utilization in the course of time.

Equity and efficiency certainly are appealing standards. They are also criteria which have usually been accepted in abstract inquiries into socialist economic merit, when these analyses have been at all rigorous. They have been accepted in such inquiries, moreover, by partisans on either side. Most often, it is true, reference is made to static efficiency, rather than to efficiency generally, but this is more a reflection on the analyses than on the dynamic standard.[3]

But, as everyone knows, Russia was a backward country not so very long ago. Is not the economic merit of Soviet socialism to be judged, therefore, primarily from the standpoint of modernization? And, granting that equity is still of interest, if any further criterion is to be used, should it not be economic growth rather than efficiency? Is this not what the Soviet government itself has been seeking above all? Is not economic growth what really matters also in less developed countries, where the choice between socialism and capitalism is chiefly an issue today?

As is not always considered, economic growth itself depends on efficiency. This is self-evident in the case of dynamic efficiency, but it is also true of static efficiency. Thus, depending on static efficiency, the community may produce a larger or smaller output with the productive factors at its disposal. Depending on such efficiency, therefore, it will be able to generate a larger or smaller surplus over any given level of consumption. Hence it can make available for capital investment a larger or smaller volume of savings. The increment of the community's output, and thus its economic growth, necessarily depends on, among other things, the volume of savings that can be made available for capital investments.

Yet, growth may also vary quite apart from efficiency. Thus, even with the same efficiency, whether static or dynamic, the supplies of productive factors may grow at varying rates. Moreover, supplies of productive factors may do so depending partly on the economic working arrangements. Most importantly, depending on the working arrangements, a community may save and add to its capital stock a larger or smaller share of the same total output. The growth of output should vary correspondingly.

Admittedly, then, so far as economic growth is prized, it represents to some extent in its own right still another standard of economic merit. And economic growth certainly has been prized in the USSR. The Soviet system's directors (as we may designate those responsible for economic policy in the USSR) have pursued many goals in economic affairs, but growth has obviously been a cardinal one.

And it is just as well to observe at once that Soviet socialism has a certain advantage from this standpoint. Under capitalism, although governments everywhere play a role, the volume of output saved is still determined largely by market forces. This is to say that savings ultimately reflect decisions of countless households and business firms. An outstanding feature of Soviet socialism is the transfer of responsibility for determination of the volume of output saved to a small group of political authorities able within wide limits to pursue such ends as they see fit.

The Soviet system's directors, thus, have had extraordinary power to determine savings. How extraordinary their power has been we may begin to infer from the use they have made of it. Under its five year plans, the Soviet government managed in an initially backward country to raise with exceptional rapidity the share of national income saved to notably high levels rarely matched in the West. As savings rose and were invested, moreover, the government also increased for long the additional share of the national income that it allocated to defense expenditures.[4]

But to achieve growth simply on this basis is necessarily to incur a cost. So far as growth is generated apart from efficiency, the inevitable corollary is material denial for consumers. The greater the growth the more the denial. Before they opt for economic working arrangements of a Soviet type in the interest of growth, therefore, those concerned with public policy in underdeveloped countries, if they are at all responsible, will wish to know what such arrangements offer in terms not only of authoritarian control over savings, but of efficiency.

Outside the socialist world, economic growth is sought, of course, not only in underdeveloped countries but in the advanced countries of the capitalist West. But in the capitalist West even those who are especially eager for growth will rarely consider authoritarian control over savings as much of a virtue.

Still, such control has obviously been a virtue to the Soviet system's directors themselves, and this must be considered if we wish to see their working arrangements from their standpoint. But I have been referring primarily to the Soviet Union under Stalin. It remains to say that since Stalin the system's directors have changed, and so too surely has their authority over, or at least their attitude towards, savings. The Soviet government through the years has promised consumers much. At long last, it has concluded that it is expedient to redeem these promises in a greater degree than it has done hitherto.

The change in the government's attitude is manifest, and need not be labored, but a corollary is not always grasped. If Soviet consumers are now to share more fully in the fruits of economic growth, economic growth is no longer achievable to the degree that it was under Stalin merely through the exaction of savings at the expense of consumption. To a greater extent than in the past, it must be achieved through efficiency.

While the corollary is not always grasped, in essentials it has been grasped by the system's directors themselves. This I take it is the deeper meaning of the measures they have taken since Stalin to improve Soviet economic performance. The much-discussed economic reforms now in progress are the chief but still only the latest of many such governmental actions. In effect, the system's directors are seeking an alternative basis for growth from that which Stalin exploited so ruthlessly.[5] (I shall have more to say later about the recent government economic measures.)

It also follows that even from the standpoint of the government, the economic merit of Soviet socialism always turned on efficiency, but it now must do so the more. By the same token, there is the more reason to appraise Soviet economic performance in terms of this standard, along with that of equity. It is already a fairly familiar fact, however, that the gains in equity due to the advent of socialism in the USSR are at best problematic. This is so according to any plausible conception of the ideal material distribution.[6] Thus, it would be difficult to add much here to what is generally known on equity in the Soviet Union. In any case, of the two standards, that of efficiency is decidedly the more novel and interesting to apply to the USSR. I shall examine the economic merit of Soviet socialism, therefore, from this standpoint.[7]

### Comparative productivity levels

Turning to this task, it is advisable for the present to focus primarily on static efficiency. This, however, is itself a many-sided category. If we are to appraise Soviet socialism at all from this standpoint, we must do so selectively.

A central aspect, however, concerns the uses made of available supplies of productive factors: land, including mineral deposits, stocks of reproducible capital, and labor of different skills. I refer to the utilization of such supplies in one or another production unit and their allocation among production units, either in the same or in different industries. Static efficiency may vary in this sphere, since, depending on the relevant working arrangements, the community may achieve very different economic results in it. Thus, depending on the working arrangements, the same production unit may function well or poorly, and so yield very different material returns to the productive factors employed. Productive factors may also move or be moved about with varying sensitivity to differences in material returns to their employment in different production units and industries. For the community generally, economic results necessarily will vary on this account as well.

Static efficiency is a rather intricate concept. These brief remarks can only suggest the nature of the aspect that is in question, but its more precise features, where they are not already familiar, will become sufficiently evident as we proceed. We need not probe further either to grasp that reference is indeed to a central facet of static efficiency. If we are able to gauge the performance of Soviet socialism in this sphere, we shall, I think, have a reasonable basis to gauge the static efficiency of this system generally. In the time available, then, it is best to focus on Soviet performance regarding uses of available productive factors within production units and their allocation among production units in the same or in different industries.

Even if we do so, appraisal of the performance of the economic system of a modern society such as that of the USSR is an ambitious project. I have assumed, I hope not wrongly, that on such an important theme even a very tentative evaluation might be of interest. I should state at once, however, what this evaluation is.

There are, I believe, significant differences in static efficiency even among Western capitalist countries. If this is so, such efficiency in the Soviet Union probably is comparable to that under capitalism where capitalism is not at its best, and perhaps where it is far from such. Certainly the Marxist claim as to the economic superiority of socialism finds no vindication here. From the standpoint of static efficiency, however, no doubt some critics have also erred by underestimating this system.

But, on a matter so difficult to gauge, conclusions are generally of less interest than the evidence on which they rest. Let me explain, then, that the evidence considered is diverse, but for the time I shall focus on some quantitative data that seem pertinent. These consist of comparative measures that have been compiled of national income or output per worker and of national income or output per unit of a composite of labor and capital, taken together. The measures have been compiled for a number of Western capitalist countries and for the Soviet Union (Table 1).

To refer first to national income per worker, for each country considered I compare performance in this respect with that of the United States. In the real terms that are of interest here, national income in two countries can be compared only if their outputs are valued in the same prices. This is also true of national income per worker. Each comparison with the United States, therefore, is made in two ways. In both the United States and the other country, output is first valued in terms of the prices of the other country and then in terms of U.S. dollars.

The results of the two sorts of computations differ and sometimes markedly so. Such "index number relativity" in global measures of production such as are in question is a predictable and by now also a fairly familiar feature. Since the structure of production differs in different countries, the system of prices in terms of which we value different products necessarily affects the comparative output aggregates that are obtained.[8]

While predictable, the discrepancy in results is also disconcerting. But note that, whichever valuation procedure is employed, the Western capitalist countries considered fall into three main groups.

First, there is the United States with the highest output per worker of all. Then there are the countries of Northwest

twenty-one

## Table 1

Real National Income per Employed Worker and per Unit of Factor Inputs, Selected Countries, 1960[a]

(USA = 100 per cent)

| | National income per employed worker | | National income per unit of factor (labor and reproducible capital) inputs | |
|---|---|---|---|---|
| | Based on foreign national price weights (1) | Based on U.S. price weights (2) | Based on foreign national price weights (3) | Based on U.S. price weights (4) |
| United States | 100 | 100 | 100 | 100 |
| Northwest Europe | 44 | 56 | 50 | 63 |
| France | 43 | 55 | 49 | 62 |
| Germany | 43 | 55 | 52 | 63 |
| United Kingdom | 44 | 56 | 50 | 63 |
| Italy | 22 | 37 | 28 | 45 |
| USSR | 22 | 38 | 28 | 45 |

[a] In comparisons of Western Europe and the United States, employment is calculated to allow for differences in annual hours, though not proportionately. In the comparison of the USSR and the United States, annual hours apparently are very similar, and no allowance is made for differences in hours worked. For sources and methods, see the Appendix.

Europe (including principally France, Germany and the United Kingdom) with per worker outputs much below that of the United States but still high. Finally, there is Italy, which in terms of output per worker falls much below all other capitalist countries.

And, whichever valuation standard is employed, the USSR stands only on a par with Italy, and below all other capitalist countries. It is also far below the United States: Soviet output per worker is but 22 to 38 per cent of the American.

Turning to national income or output per composite unit of labor and capital, calculations of the sort in question lately have often been made in economics, but they are not yet widely familiar. Their nature and deeper rationale are by now the subject of a sizable technical literature. It suffices here, however, to consider that the aim is to measure the comparative productivity, not of labor alone, but of labor and capital, taken together. This is done by comparing for pairs of countries levels of output with levels of inputs of the two factors. For each country the level of inputs is represented essentially by the total cost of the two factors employed. Costs are calculated at charges for each factor that either prevail in the market or may be imputed to the input. The factor charges in question, of course, ordinarily will differ in the two countries compared, but alternative computations are made of comparative levels of inputs in the two countries in terms of alternative charges. This is done in just the same way as outputs in two countries are compared first in terms of the prices of one and then in terms of the prices of the other country.[9]

Reason to include capital in the calculation of productivity is that we are interested in efficiency of economic working arrangements. When calculated for labor alone, productivity may vary between countries not because of differences in efficiency of such working arrangements, but because of differences in the supply of capital available to cooperate with the labor. Output per worker may be higher in one country than another simply because each worker is equipped with more capital in the former country. Working arrangements

twenty-three

for using both factors together need not be at all superior. With the inclusion of capital in our calculations we in effect allow for such differences in its supply.

As before, for each country considered I compare performance with that of the United States. Also in both the United States and the other country, output and input costs are calculated first in terms of the prices of the other country and then in terms of U.S. dollar prices. As before, too, the measure of productivity obtained for any country depends on the valuation procedure employed. Whichever the procedure, however, output per worker does in fact vary among the countries we consider because of differences in capital supply. But only in part. After the inclusion of capital, productivity varies less than before between countries, but it still varies widely. Moreover, among Western capitalist countries, the United States still stands at the top of our list. The countries of Northwest Europe still stand in the middle, and Italy remains at the bottom. And the USSR is still comparable only with Italy. Its output per unit of factor inputs is but 28 to 45 per cent of the American.

### Sources of productivity differentials

In compiling the data that have been presented, I have drawn on the results of a considerable volume of research, by others as well as myself. Yet, index number relativity apart, comparative data of the sort in question are unlikely to be precisely accurate. Even the less initiated scarcely need be told this. The data that have been compiled here are no exception to this rule, and must be read accordingly. Among other things, we must not take very literally the almost exact equality of our measures for the USSR and Italy. Our data are much too crude for that.

Furthermore, in judging from these data the efficiency of Soviet working arrangements we have yet to consider some further complexities where measurement is often still more difficult. But with all their limitations the data, I still feel, tend to support my conclusion as to the undistinguished performance of Soviet socialism.

As for the complexities, these arise from the fact that the efficiency of economic working arrangements is closely related to but not the same thing as productivity. In other words, there are economic factors other than efficiency that affect our productivity measures. There are such factors even after we allow, as we have, for differences in capital stock. Even in a summary account we must consider several of the factors in question. To begin with, labor may vary in quality among different countries. Because of such variation, productivity too may vary without economic working arrangements necessarily being at all at fault. Hence efficiency need not be any the less in one case than in another.

Where labor quality differs, however, two principal reasons must be differences in the level of education of the labor force and varying rates of employment of female workers. We owe to Dr. Denison an ingenious method for determining the importance for productivity of differences in education levels and female employment rates.[10] This method involves reference to differentials in earnings among workers of different educational levels and sex. The method is admittedly quite inexact.

But it is still illuminating to apply it to allow for differences in educational levels and female employment rates here. Thus, in terms of comparative productivity, Northwest Europe and Italy now gain on the United States (Table 2). The USSR gains also and to a greater extent, but it still falls below all Western capitalist countries except Italy. Thus the Soviet output per worker is still but 29 to 48 per cent, and its output per unit of factor inputs but 34 to 56 per cent of the American.

The calculations in question entail discounting female labor in all countries by 41 per cent. This conforms to the average difference in earnings between male and female workers in the United States. This differential presumably often reflects limitations in employment opportunities open to women rather than the inherent ineffectiveness of their labor. One may perhaps feel that this is so even without being a feminist. So far as it is, the calculation tends to be unduly favorable to the USSR. In the Soviet Union, women are employed to a greater

twenty-five

Table 2

Real National Income per Employed Worker and per Unit of Factor Inputs, with Employment Adjusted for Labor Quality, Selected Countries, 1960[a]

(USA = 100 per cent)

| | National income per employed worker | | National income per unit of factor (labor and re-producible capital) inputs | |
|---|---|---|---|---|
| | Based on foreign na-tional price weights (1) | Based on U.S. price weights (2) | Based on foreign na-tional price weights (3) | Based on U.S. price weights (4) |
| United States | 100 | 100 | 100 | 100 |
| Northwest Europe | 47 | 60 | 53 | 67 |
| France | 47 | 60 | 53 | 66 |
| Germany | 47 | 61 | 56 | 69 |
| United Kingdom | 47 | 60 | 52 | 66 |
| Italy | 26 | 44 | 32 | 52 |
| USSR | 29 | 48 | 34 | 56 |

[a] For sources and methods, see the Appendix.

degree than in any other country considered. They now constitute one-half of the Soviet labor force. In the West the corresponding figure is one-fourth to one-third. An inordinately high discount for female labor necessarily would inflate calculated productivity for the USSR relative to that for other countries.[11]

For labor, I have been referring to employment rather than the total supply available, including unemployment. The government of the USSR has long claimed that it has abolished unemployment there. In fact, "frictional unemployment" necessarily continues on some scale, but the magnitude is speculative. In the West, unemployment has varied in any one country and as between countries. But in recent post-war years it usually has remained within relatively narrow limits. With unemployment included in the labor supply, our measures of productivity for the USSR might rise a few percent relative to the United States. They probably would rise little, if at all, relatively to most Western European countries.[12]

Whether calculated for labor alone or for labor and capital together, productivity may also vary among different countries because of differences in supplies of mineral resources and usable agricultural land. Again the variation could be quite apart from differences in efficiency of economic working arrangements. As a country of continental dimensions, the USSR is by all accounts well-endowed with mineral resources, and should not be at any consequential disadvantage in this regard. As for agricultural land, where climatic factors are considered, this is inferior in quality in the Soviet Union, at least by U.S. standards. But the inferior Soviet quality is offset by cultivation of a larger area. Inclusion in our calculations of agricultural land as still another factor input would not seem to affect the results materially.[13]

Efficiency of working arrangements apart, productivity might also vary because of differences in market size, and in the opportunities thus provided for exploitation of economies of scale. Size of the market is not the same thing as size of the country, for transportation costs and freedom of access to foreign buyers also matter. But the USSR should be at no disadvantage at this point. Indeed, regarding market size it probably has an advantage relative to all the Western capitalist countries considered except the United States.

Our concern now is primarily with efficiency of the static sort. This is understood to be such that a country would receive a perfect grade in it if it should exploit fully economic opportunities opened to it by available knowledge of production technologies. Available technological knowledge, however, may differ in different countries. So far as it does, such a difference too can be expected to affect productivity. Here again, therefore, productivity may vary among countries without corresponding variation in static efficiency.

But, while this must be considered along with other complexities already mentioned, it could easily be overrated. Thus, if a country's accumulated stock of technological knowledge should be relatively limited, this presumably is due to persistent deficiencies in its working arrangements for acquiring such knowledge. Such deficiencies come under the heading of dynamic rather than static efficiency, but differences in productivity on their account would still indicate differences in efficiency generally. For present purposes, this is hardly to the bad.

But may not a country's stock of technological knowledge be relatively limited even apart from deficiencies in working arrangements for its acquisition, at least of any recent date? What, for example, if for historical reasons one country should have begun to industrialize on any scale later than another and had accumulated a smaller stock of technological knowledge simply on this account? Is this not likely to be true of the USSR in particular?

A latecomer to industrialization might indeed find it difficult even at best fully to match its more advanced rivals regarding the stock of technological knowledge. But if the latecomer has had some time to progress, and if it has functioned at all effectively during this period, the shortfall in technological knowledge should be very modest. After all, production technologies are not easily monopolized. Those that have been developed in one country may very often be borrowed by another, if not at once, at least after a limited interval. Moreover, heavy reliance on borrowing from abroad is likely to be economically expedient at an early stage of industrialization when engineering and scientific resources are limited. But domestic creativity should normally become increasingly important as development proceeds. With this, any shortfall in the latecomer's stock of technological knowledge should be the more limited.

As for the USSR, I shall inquire later into dynamic efficiency there, including performance in the acquisition of new technological knowledge. Suffice it to observe now that, however good or bad such performance has been, the Soviet Union has been a late-comer in industrialization. As such it necessarily has relied heavily on borrowing from abroad for the acquisition of new technologies.

The USSR, however, initiated its First Five Year Plan in 1928. It has thus had a number of decades to raise its stock of technological knowledge to the level of the capitalist West. If not through domestic innovation, it could still do so through borrowing from abroad. If the USSR should still be at a material disadvantage regarding available technological knowledge, it must be agreed, I think, that the preponderant cause must be, not the late start, but inefficiency. This must be so even where the Soviet stock of technological knowledge is compared with that of the United States. But it must be even more the case where it is compared with that in Western Europe. As measures of efficiency, therefore, our comparative data can be subject to little distortion at this point.[14]

Measurements of productivity of a composite of factors as well as of labor alone are by now a familiar feature in economics. Their use, however, as a basis to compare efficiency of different social systems is still relatively novel. Even so, it seems possible to gauge broadly the diverse complexities involved, but with further research it may be hoped that we shall gain further insight into this important matter.

twenty-nine

## Output structure

We have been seeking to gauge the efficiency of working arrangements in the USSR for determining uses of available supplies of productive factors. So far as our comparative data on productivity bear on this matter, however, they relate to performance in respect of total output. What of the structure of such output? How have the Soviet working arrangements performed in this respect?

Among the goods included in national product, many, such as machinery and factory structures, are intended primarily to produce other goods of a more final nature. Regarding output structure, therefore, efficiency must turn ultimately on the proportions in which such more final goods are produced. Among these supplies, the bulk necessarily consist of consumers' goods. The structure of production of these goods is to be discussed at a later point, but I may anticipate a major finding: At least in respect of quality and assortment, the Soviet bill of consumers' goods must diverge far from any that might be optimal. The bill of consumers' goods produced in Western capitalist countries also has its limitations, but it could hardly be as dubious as that in the USSR.[15]

## Conclusions

I have already stated the conclusion to which our inquiry seems to lead: as exemplified by the USSR, socialism is by no means a superior system from the standpoint of static efficiency. It may function as well as capitalism, however, when capitalism is not performing very well. I have focused on the comparative performance of Soviet socialism and Western capitalism, but have assumed that there are differences in static efficiency even among capitalist countries. Our inquiry seems incidentally to support this plausible supposition.

But I have considered thus far only part of the evidence available on Soviet static efficiency, and we must reserve judgment on this matter until we can approach it in another illuminating way, particularly by examining the sources of Soviet inefficiency. This is the subject of my next lecture, however, and I must defer comment on it until then.

November 2, 1967

## II. Sources of inefficiency

# II. Sources of inefficiency

## Introduction

The theme of these lectures is the economic merit of socialism as found in the USSR. The standard of economic merit that is considered is efficiency. In my first lecture I explored this matter in the light of data on comparative levels of productivity in the USSR and Western capitalist countries. Such data bear especially on efficiency of the static sort. This, it will be recalled, is the degree to which, equity apart, the community is able to realize an economic optimum in exploiting the material opportunities that available technological knowledge opens to it. This, is, of course, an ideal that no economic system in the real world can fully attain. Under Western capitalism the shortfall from the ideal originates in diverse causes which surely must often be rather consequential. One need not have mastered all the analytic intricacies involved to be aware of this. What are the more significant sources of static inefficiency under socialism and how do they compare with those under Western capitalism?

In theoretic inquiries that have been made into the economic merit of socialism, a principal concern has been to explore just this question. If in the light of such abstract speculation we now inquire into the sources of static inefficiency in the USSR, we may gain further insight into the comparative extent of such waste there. We may do so, I think, even though the available evidence on sources of static efficiency in the USSR is largely qualitative, rather than quantitative.

An inquiry into sources of static inefficiency almost inevitably tends to become something of a critique. The one which we are now undertaking will be no exception to this rule. Perhaps I should explain, therefore, that Western scholarly research on the Soviet economy, which serves as a point of departure in these lectures generally, is by now relatively advanced regarding sources of static inefficiency. If I am engaged in a critique, then, it may be hoped that the critique is not a merely subjective one.

After many five year plans, industry has come to occupy a central place in the Soviet economy. Moreover, the working arrangements for determining uses of productive factors in industry often have a counterpart in other sectors. At any rate, in exploring sources of static inefficiency in the USSR, we may properly, I think, refer especially to industry.

As understood here, socialism obtains in the Soviet Union so far as ownership of the means of production is primarily public. Indeed in the USSR such ownership is almost universally public. This is true above all in industry. Even so, however, industrial life might still be organized in various ways. How it has been organized in the Soviet Union is generally known, at least in broad outline. Three basic features should be kept in mind here.

The first is the pervasive bureaucracy. To a notable degree, means of production are administered through a complex of bureaucratic structures, each culminating in the Council of Ministers in Moscow. Second, there is the all-embracing complex of plans that are supposed to be guiding. The most famous of these is the five year plan, the first of which went into effect in October 1928. The five year plan, however, and other plans that are formulated for even longer periods are reflected finally in a plan for a single year. This annual plan bears most immediately on current operations.

Third and last, but not least, is the centralization of decision-making. The agency immediately in charge of operations, the publicly owned "enterprise" (*predpriiatie*), necessarily has a certain autonomy. As we shall see, this autonomy is important. But to a striking extent agencies superior to the enterprise coordinate and direct economic affairs everywhere. They do so, furthermore, not so much indirectly through manipulation of prices and other financial instruments, as by entering directly into the physical process itself, that is by the fixing of physical quotas and the like.

Under socialism, a system of economic administration with these three features is usually referred to as "centralist planning." I shall observe this usage here.

thirty-three

## Industrial labor effort

Turning to sources of inefficiency in industry (I refer, of course, to the static variety, and unless otherwise indicated efficiency and inefficiency will continue to be so understood), these are to be found partly in the functioning of the enterprise and partly in the functioning of superior agencies. I shall begin with the enterprise, and consider first an aspect that is usually neglected in economic texts. As I need not tell this audience, however, it is important. I refer to the worker's attitude towards labor, as it bears on his preferences between labor effort and earnings.

Unhappily, this is also elusive. Thus, so far as capitalism functions with varying efficiency in different countries, it is often suggested that national differences in the workers' preferences between effort and earnings must be a significant cause. More particularly, one of the reasons why the United States surpasses Western Europe in efficiency is said to be simply that, other things equal, the American industrial worker is inclined to work more diligently than his European counterpart.

Very possibly he is, but differences in attitude such as are in question are difficult to demonstrate. Furthermore, so far as they exist, they should result in differences in productivity. But, to repeat, efficiency of economic working arrangements is not entirely the same thing as productivity. This is true here as elsewhere. Thus, in order to conclude that efficiency varies because of differences in labor attitude, the economist would wish to know whether attitudes inducing greater effort in one country than another were in some sense more satisfying to the worker. They must often be so. At least, one is led to speculate that they are when he inquires into the complex psychological factors that may inhibit effort — a subject which distinguished colleagues at this institution have helped illuminate.[1] But attitudes inducing greater effort need not be more satisfying, and if they are not it would be difficult to conclude from the international differences in productivity more than that capitalism simply gratifies differing preferences between effort and earnings in different countries, just as it gratifies differing preferences among different consumers' goods. In the one case no more than in the other would the differences in tastes signify a difference in efficiency.

We are concerned, however, not so much with the comparative efficiency of capitalism in different countries where this system prevails as with the efficiency of socialism relative to that of capitalism. Here it has been urged not only that there must be a difference in the workers' attitude towards labor, but that the difference could be of a relatively profound sort. This has been urged, that is, by socialists.

Thus the knowledge that with common ownership of the means of production, every value he creates "ultimately redounds to the benefit of himself, his own kind and class," it has been held, will almost inevitably be the basis for a deep transformation in the worker's attitude towards labor. Just what the new socialist attitude that emerges will be is not always very clear, but it is manifestly to be of a sort favorable to service generally, and hence to effort and productivity. One is led to suppose that the new attitude would also be more satisfying to the worker, and so be favorable to efficiency.[2]

This is also a theory about which anyone who is not a socialist is apt to be skeptical. But the question at issue is weighty. In inquiring into the sources of inefficiency in the USSR we should be wrong not to pause and consider whether that country may not have an advantage at this point. I should explain, therefore, that the worker's attitude towards labor in the Soviet Union is just as elusive as that elsewhere. Even so, however, if a transformation in that attitude that is at all profound has occurred, it is surprisingly difficult to detect.

Thus, consider the Soviet government's policy on the differentiation of money wages. The policy is already broadly familiar. I had it in mind in commenting earlier on the doubtful nature of any gains in equity that socialism has brought to the USSR. Essentially, the system's directors have seen fit to continue to pay differential rewards to labor on much the same basis as under capitalism (that is, according to arduousness, skill, responsibility, and the like). At least for workers of lesser rank, the differentials in earnings are also of a magnitude not by any means inferior to those often encountered in the capitalist West.[3] If the Soviet workers' attitude towards labor should have been transformed as suggested, the government imaginably might still have found it in order to differentiate material rewards for labor in this way, but this seems quite improbable.

I said that the differentiation of wages is similar to that under capitalism. Actually the government has deviated somewhat from capitalism in one important sphere, but in a way which makes the assumed transformation in labor attitude appear even less likely than before. I refer to the use of piecework. Of factory workers in the United States, less than 30 per cent are paid by the piece. Piece-work is used more extensively than this in some Western European countries, but I believe rarely to the degree in the USSR, where as many as 60 per cent of the industrial workers have recently been paid by the piece.[4]

The Soviet government admittedly has not been unconcerned with labor psychology. Nor has it been content to await passively the change in the worker's attitude that public ownership under socialism supposedly would bring. Rather, it has consciously sought to hasten this process at every opportunity. With its control over education, the press, the arts and culture generally, the government's opportunities have been many. The government has not hesitated, either, to expound for the worker the particular imperatives of socialist life appropriate to each and every occasion. A compendium of the slogans thus enunciated would be voluminous indeed.

It would be surprising, however, if the worker should not have been resistant to the transformation in attitude that the government has sought to foster. It would be surprising in view of the government's policies on the allocation of output between capital investment and consumption that I have already referred to, in view of the manner of determining the consumption structure, which I have also already mentioned and on which I shall soon have more to say, and in view also of dark currents in Soviet political life that are too familiar to need elaboration here.

Even so, we must not discount altogether the special force under socialism of a concern to serve as a factor inducing labor effort in the USSR. The Soviet worker surely has often exerted himself more on this account than he might have otherwise. One need only delve into Soviet history to become convinced of this.

But the reservoir of socialist idealism on which the government has thus been able to draw was by all accounts at a peak in early years. The war apart, it has dwindled ever since. By how much it has done so, we may perhaps judge from the words which a Soviet playwright has recently had one of his characters speak; a Soviet playwright, it should be observed, who has experienced all of the five year plans as an adult:[5]

> I am sick of being a bridge between the old and the new world. I no longer want to go around with a sore and bloody back. Let me rest . . . I am tired of struggling . . . struggling in science . . . struggling for bread . . . struggling for atomic energy . . . struggling for the development of virgin land. Even for a quiet rest, it is necessary to struggle. That's enough struggle for me! Give me a chance just to live as a human being.

Among those who have urged that public ownership under socialism would transform the workers' attitude towards labor, not least was Marx. Marx, however, considered that the change in attitude would occur, not on the morrow of the Revolution, but only in the course of time. This was in part the basis for his famous distinction between the two phases of socialism, the one following immediately after the Revolution and the other to be achieved only at a later stage.[6] Even so, Marx himself perhaps would have been disappointed by the limited progress in transforming the worker's attitude that has been made thus far in the Soviet Union.

I have been referring to the worker's attitude towards labor as this bears on his preferences between effort and wages generally, rather than to the specific choice the worker makes at any time between these aspects. Such a choice between effort and wages depends not only on preferences generally but on the particular material incentives that prevail. Our more basic concern, however, is with efficiency. Must we not consider then that even if a new socialist attitude towards labor has not emerged in the USSR, labor effort still is impaired under capitalism because material incentives are often defective? And have not the Russians been able to score at least here? Specifically, so far as piece-work is more widely used in the Soviet Union, would not this in itself be to the good from the standpoint of efficiency?

Even from this standpoint, piece-work may easily be employed to excess. Thus, because of the technology employed, for example, under some conveyor systems, the worker may have little control over output. In such circumstances use of piece-work may be rather footless. This apparently has often been the case in the USSR. The cited figure on Soviet workers paid by the piece already reflects a reduction from earlier peak levels. The reduction was made in part because, as the government has come to realize, piece-work has often been employed where it is technologically inappropriate. The government may find it in order to restrict application of this system still further in future.[7]

Where technologically admissible, piece-work may still not always be especially favorable to efficiency. At least, it has not always been so in the USSR. For example, labor effort supposedly is stimulated by use of this system, but the Soviet worker understandably has tended to limit his exertions in periods preceding an anticipated review of output norms. This is acknowledged by Soviet economists.[8] Again, I shall refer later to the production of goods of inferior quality, a persuasive feature of the Soviet economic scene. The extensive employment of piece work is clearly one of the reasons for this costly phenomenon. In brief, efficiency in the USSR may have benefited from widespread use of piece-work there, but this has yet to be demonstrated. Incidentally, the Soviet worker's tendency to restrict effort on the eve of a review of piece-work norms and to produce defective goods would seem to illuminate further the limited extent of any socialist transformation that has occurred in his attitude towards labor.

Material incentives for labor effort have many dimensions of which the use or non-use of piece-work is only one. Piece-work aside, therefore, the Russians may sometimes have an advantage regarding material incentives, but if so this is not clear. At least in one respect the advantage must lie rather with the West. I refer to the impact of taxes on labor effort. So far as they are borne by the worker, taxes of any conventional sort in any system limit the real return to effort. They thus tend also to impair efficiency. The precise way in which this occurs is not always fully understood, but the essential point is evident and this suffices here.

By implication, the financing of public expenditures must impair labor effort almost everywhere, but it would be surprising if the impairment were not relatively marked in a country such as the USSR: a country, that is, where the government has assumed notably large fiscal responsibilities, including provision of much of the funds that are required to finance the vast investments it projects in its pursuit of rapid growth, and where as a result taxes bear especially heavily on the worker's real earnings. Thus, the chief source of revenue in the USSR is the notorious turnover tax. Because of this levy, Soviet retail prices in 1960 averaged 52 per cent above levels corresponding to factor charges.[9]

*Enterprise management*

In discussing labor effort under Soviet socialism as compared with that under Western capitalism, I have by implication already become somewhat involved with the management of the Soviet public enterprise, on the one hand, and of the capitalist business enterprise, on the other. Material incentives are, of course, a cardinal responsibility of management in the West, and in a degree management of the Soviet enterprise also has authority in this sphere. Such incentives apart,

thirty-nine

under Western capitalism, if the worker's attitude towards labor is faulty, management is rarely blameless. This is also true in the Soviet enterprise. What, however, of the comparative performance of Soviet enterprise management more generally?

In the sphere of management, it is widely assumed that Western capitalism is often at its best, or nearly so, economically. I have no desire to challenge this assumption in any serious way, but even one who is favorably impressed must be aware that under the most skilled management the enterprise may still be a source of inefficiency in the economy generally. It may be such, that is, if it has monopoly power, or if it generates extra-market social values or costs. Factory smoke is the classic example of such extra-market effects, but needless to say there are many others.

Monopoly power and extra-market effects apart, the primers still teach, as Adam Smith did, that in seeking profit management also serves the cause of efficiency in the economy generally. In the real world of Western capitalism, however, management often seeks diverse goals of which profit is only one. Whether efficiency is always well served thereby, it is generally understood, is at least doubtful. Then, too, given its goals, capitalist management is often particularly impressive in the administration of the enterprise's internal affairs. But even here, whether because of weakness of competition or for other reasons, "best practice" managerial procedures do not seem always to be disseminated and applied nearly as quickly or as widely as they might. Efficiency tends to suffer, therefore, on this account as well.

These limitations obtain under Western capitalism everywhere, but it is often argued that, through their varying incidence, they contribute to observed differences in efficiency in different capitalist countries, particularly between the USA and Western Europe. This is certainly plausible, though not easy to demonstrate conclusively.

But, in reminding you of the limitations of enterprise management in the West, I do not wish at all to suggest that such management in the USSR performs better. On the contrary, as it turns out Soviet enterprise management too has its limitations. Under centralist planning, these are often rather different from those affecting enterprise management in the West. Their comparative importance is also difficult to gauge. But the deficiencies of Soviet enterprise management are obviously consequential.

That Soviet enterprise management leaves something to be desired is no secret in the Soviet Union. Especially in recent years, deficiencies of such management have been the subject of continuing public criticism. The deficiencies by now have also been commented on widely in the West.

I need refer, therefore, only to bare essentials.[10] To begin with, there is the notorious "safety factor": plan targets are formulated by superior agencies, but contrary to a common assumption not exclusively by them. Almost inevitably, the management of the enterprise also participates. In practice what takes place, therefore, is often more nearly negotiation than mere direction from above. Almost inevitably, too, managerial personnel, whose success is judged by and who receive bonuses in proportion to the degree of fulfillment of plan targets, seek to limit these goals so that their fulfillment will be easier. The management is also frequently reluctant to overfulfill targets. Such overfulfillment could be the basis for pressure from above for still higher goals in the future.

Managerial success is judged and bonuses are paid on the basis of fulfillment of plan targets generally, but one target, or some variant thereof, has long been primary. This is the target for the enterprise's gross output. This gives rise to further oddities.

Thus, in order to fulfill the target for gross output, enterprise managers often find it possible and also expedient to stress inordinately goods that bulk large physically. Alternatively, where gross output is calculated in value terms, managers may emphasize products that have relatively high ruble prices. Such prices also have their limitations, however, so the resulting assortment again may be strange. How much so we may readily judge from the unending complaints of consumers themselves, complaints, for example, about the availability of small-sized men's shoes but not large-sized boys' shoes, of expensive but not cheap dishware, of light household, as distinct from other enamelware, and so on.

Despite special controls, managers also find it in order to sacrifice quality for quantity. This too might have been expected, but it is still surprising to learn that among products examined in the first half of 1962 by inspectors of the Ministry of Trade of the Russian Republic, 33 per cent of clothing articles had to be rejected or reclassified in a lower quality category. This was also the fate of 25 per cent of knitwear and 33 per cent of leather shoes. Among clothing and knitwear articles inspected by the Ministry of Trade of the Ukraine during 1963, 20 to 25 per cent had to be condemned as defective. Should you ever happen to be subjected to a dull Soviet documentary film, you may be interested to know that even here defective success criteria are a factor: as *Pravda* tells us, studios simply find it remunerative to produce two mediocre films rather than to take pains to produce one good one.

A distorted assortment and defective quality are, as the examples suggest, all too familiar in the case of consumers' goods. For the more favored basic industrial goods, such deficiencies should be less frequent, but it is not very difficult to find examples here as well: such as that of the Rostov Farm Machinery Plant which in a five year period was compelled, because of deficiencies in deliveries by suppliers, to make 11,000 substitutions of rolled metal shapes and dimensions; or that of the Minsk Machinery Plant, one-third of the output of which was found to be defective.

In order to fulfill the current target for gross output, managers are also prone to avoid interruptions in production operations that might be required to assure adequate repair of machinery. According to a long-standing practice, much of the enterprise's fixed capital is made available to it in the form of interest-free grants from the government budget. For this reason, managerial interest in proper maintenance is somewhat attentuated in any event. Because of uncertainties regarding supply, managers also hoard scarce materials, which thereby become still scarcer; so that it is not at all unknown for enterprises to be holding several years' supply of one or another critically-short material. The list of aberrations of Soviet enterprise management could easily be extended still further.

I have been discussing aberrations in Soviet enterprise management induced by the criteria used to test and reward managerial success. It is only fair to say that another and rather different cause of inefficiency in the enterprise appears to be no longer as important as it once was. I refer to the selection of managers chiefly on the basis of their political, as distinct from professional, qualifications. But, while the era of the Red Director is long since past, managers are still expected to be party members. It would be surprising if, even now, professional competence should not sometimes be sacrificed for politics.

In theoretic discussions of the economic merit of socialism, advocates of this system almost always assume that, in contrast to the managers of the capitalist business enterprise, those administering the socialist public enterprises could be relied on to serve effectively the public interest. For their part, critics of socialism not surprisingly have demurred at this. Deficiencies such as have been observed in Soviet managerial behavior, I believe, if anything, go much beyond any anticipated on an abstract plane even by critics. Under Soviet socialism, a "visible" hand has replaced Adam Smith's "invisible" one. But the enterprise apparently still does not always serve the country's interests. Indeed, it very often behaves quite otherwise.

In examining sources of inefficiency within the Soviet enterprise, I have now considered labor effort as this is affected by the worker's attitude and material incentives. I have also considered managerial behavior. What of trade unions? Under Western capitalism, do these not impair not only labor effort but efficiency generally? And so far as trade unions have been made subservient to the government in the USSR, would not the Russians have an important advantage at least here?

One of the ways in which unions are supposed to impair efficiency in the West is through opposition to piece-work. Union attitudes towards piece-work under capitalism probably are more complex than often is assumed, but admittedly such organizations have not been able to restrict application of piece-work in the Soviet Union. But I have already commented on the possible consequencies for efficiency in the Soviet Union of the relatively extensive use of piece-work there. Hence I will say no more on this matter now.

Piece-work apart, under Western capitalism unions manifestly do tend often to limit efficiency. But the plant environment which they help establish may also have some virtues from this standpoint. So at least less partisan students of this involved subject appear to feel, and we must see accordingly the impact of unions on efficiency.[11]

As for trade unions in the USSR, according to the doctrine long accepted there, given public ownership of the means of production, there necessarily is no possibility of class conflict such as prevails under capitalism. It also follows that there is no place for unions which would seek to represent the workers in such a conflict.

Yet trade unions do exist. Some of their functions, it is true, are rather novel, such as that of enlisting the worker's "creative initiative," but some are of a more conventional kind. Moreover, the unions are certainly subservient to the government, but the government has found it expedient at least lately to try to assure that they should not be entirely subservient to enterprise management as well. Thus, unions have authority and seem often genuinely to represent the worker's interests in disputes over dismissals and similar matters.[12]

That efficiency would be favored under socialism as a result of change in the status and role of trade unions has often been claimed by advocates of such a society. This has also been contended, if anything even more emphatically, by some critics of socialism.[13] In the Soviet Union efficiency probably has benefited at this point, though I suspect not as much as proponents and critics alike have suggested.

*Coordination and direction by superior agencies*

In exploring sources of efficiency in Soviet industry, I have focused thus far on the enterprise. To turn to superior agencies, these have the task of coordinating and directing different enterprises, and economic affairs generally. Under Western capitalism, the analogous function is performed largely not by anyone in particular, but by the market. Which is more efficient at this point, Western capitalism or Soviet socialism?

While socialists since Marx almost never fail to refer to the capitalist market as a form of anarchy, at least the more sophisticated have understood that the anarchy conceals a notable degree of order. Yet the capitalist market has its limitations. No one will dispute this, and deeper inquiry seems only to underline the obvious in disclosing that the resultant inefficiency must often be significant.

Suffice it to recall that, while extremes of business depression seem a thing of the past, cyclical fluctuations with their attendant misdirection and underutilization of resources still are with us, and that even apart from such fluctuations complete market equilibrium of any basic sort must be rather rare. Governmental actions, while no doubt often contributing to stability generally, may also be a source of inefficiency, as in the case of incentive-impairing taxes, farm restrictions, tariffs, and the like.

What of Soviet socialism? In abstract discussions, many protagonists of socialism seem to take it as almost self-evident that, with the institution of planning, this system will be especially advantageous in respect of coordination and direction. Others have elaborated at length on this theme, but still arrive at the same agreeable conclusion.

For their part, however, critics of socialism have advanced a rebuttal that has become famous. In trying to supersede the capitalist market, it is reasoned, superior agencies under socialism must assume vast responsibilities, with which they cannot possibly grapple effectively. Such agencies are thus bound again and again to act arbitrarily, or at least uneconomically, if they are able to act at all. While the capitalist market has its limitations, therefore, inefficiency in coordination and direction will hardly be absent under socialism. Indeed, the result there may well be chaos.

In the Soviet Union, the task of superior agencies is in fact formidable. Under centralist planning, such agencies must determine in essentials the volume and direction of investment for the country generally. They also have major responsibility for the coordination of myriads of plan targets, and exercise substantial control over inputs of productive factors, especially of materials, fuel, power, and machinery, that are needed to implement the plan in each and every enterprise.

Not surprisingly, this is also a task with which the superior agencies have found it difficult to cope. As a source of inefficiency in the functioning of these agencies, however, the formidable nature of their task has only been compounded by another factor not so clearly predicted in theoretic discussion even by critics. I refer to the strange economic principles which the superior agencies seem often to apply. These are the principles that are founded on the labor theory of value that Marx espoused. This obsolete theory continues to mold Soviet economic thought and practice, though not as much as in the past. Efficiency has also been adversely affected by still another factor that was unanticipated in theory, though it is not easy to disentangle this from other causes. This is the disdain for, if not hostility toward economic principles generally that is found among many in authority. This too is not as important as it was in the era of the "cult of personality," but continuing complaints in the USSR must be read at least partly in this light.[14] Indeed, as will appear, such an attitude is by no means an accidental feature of Soviet centralist planning.

Under socialism, critics have argued, superior agencies will be especially hampered because of their inability to fix prices that conform to "scarcity values." There can thus be no satisfactory basis for economic calculation. The dubious nature of the ruble prices of industrial goods is by now almost a legend even in the USSR. Superior agencies manifestly have been handicapped at almost every turn on this account. For superior agencies to calculate on the basis of such distorted ruble prices has not been easy; but it has been no easier for them to calculate without them.

But while, as was forecast, dubious prices have been a major source of difficulty, here too the deeper causes at work are somewhat more complex than was predicted on an abstract plane. Thus, if prices of industrial goods in the USSR diverge from scarcity values, this is certainly due in part to the sheer bureaucratic inertia in the face of an enormously difficult task. Such inertia is manifest everywhere, but perhaps nowhere more clearly than in the tendency to revise prices only very infrequently and as part of a general price reform. The last such reform was carried out as long ago as July 1955!

But prices also diverge from scarcity values for other reasons. Thus, it is Marx's labor theory of value rather than the magnitude of the task of superior agencies that accounts for another notable defect of Soviet industrial price formation: the failure at any time to account for interest on fixed capital and rent on scarce natural resources.[15]

How inefficient have superior agencies been? If we may judge at all from observed behavioral patterns[16] surely to an imposing degree, though no doubt still not quite as much as some of the more vigorous critics have contended. I refer to behavioral patterns such as the tendency described by a distinguished Soviet economist, A. Birman, for the "center" to proceed in its planning work "from average conditions that did not exist in reality in any one enterprise" and to add "an approximate average rate of growth, which was low for some and intolerable for other enterprises"; the failure for long to subject new investments to any interest test and the inability, now that the so-called "coefficient of effectiveness" calculation is employed, to settle on any meaningful standard coefficient, or to find any satisfactory solution to the problem posed by the fact that the calculation of investment effectiveness is in the dubious ruble prices, with the inevitable result that different productive factors again and again are combined in disproportionate amounts; the related inability to formulate and adhere to any satisfactory criterion for plant size, and the associated commitment at different times to economically grotesque "giants," which not very surprisingly have often coexisted with no less grotesque "pygmies"; and the chronic difficulties in completing new capacity and in utilizing such capacity fully after its completion. (Even in such key branches as chemicals and aluminum, for example, reported utilization rates have been as low as 17 and 32 per cent one to two years after new plant capacity was introduced.)

I also refer to the volume of red tape enveloping any and all operations which sometimes must set something of a record, as where requisitions for ball bearings by one auto factory had to be processed by fourteen agencies and generated some 430 pounds of documents, while a director of a metal works had to submit in the course of half a year to 445 inspections by staff of the Committee of People's Control, staff incidentally, who reportedly number in the "millions."

## Conclusions

I undertook to examine sources of inefficiency in the USSR in order to gain further insight into the extent of inefficiency there. The evidence on sources tends to be qualitative, and is not easily summarized, but the resultant waste manifestly could be sizable. Our inquiry, therefore, does not seem inconsistent with the finding suggested by comparative data previously presented on Soviet productivity: in terms of efficiency, Soviet socialism is to be compared with capitalism, but with this system when it is not nearly at its best.

In inquiring into sources of inefficiency, it is true, I have focused on industry. But, to repeat, working arrangements elsewhere in the economy are often much the same as in industry. Moreover, the chief sector of the Soviet economy aside from industry is agriculture. Here the working arrangements are admittedly rather special. Most importantly, cooperative as distinct from public ownership is still the order of the day, though not as much so as formerly.

The notorious collective farm, however, bears only a remote resemblance to cooperatives known in the West. No one needs to be told in any case that Soviet collective farm agriculture also has its failings. Just what these are perhaps is not always clearly grasped, and it is not always considered either that working arrangements for agriculture under Western capitalism also leave something to be desired from the standpoint of efficiency. Recall, for example, our own governmental restrictions on production. But it is already sufficiently evident, and I don't think requires demonstration, that in agriculture as well as industry Soviet socialism functions in a manner consistent with the view of its efficiency I have advanced.[17]

Indeed, so far as Soviet socialism is inefficient, it sometimes is suggested that this is due chiefly to defects of this system in agriculture rather than in the economy generally. The collectivized agriculture of the USSR certainly has its limitations, but as we have seen deficiencies are by no means absent elsewhere.

Still, our comparative data on productivity related to the economy as a whole, including agriculture. It should be observed, therefore, that according to a preliminary computation, productivity in the Soviet Union compares more favorably with that in the United States for non-farm sectors alone than for the economy as a whole. The margin between the two countries, however, is still very wide. Thus, national income per employed worker in the USSR was found previously to be 22 to 38 per cent of that in the United States. The corresponding relation for non-farm sectors alone is 27 to 50 per cent. Soviet national income per unit of factor input was found before to be 28 to 45 per cent of the American. The corresponding relation for non-farm sectors alone is 32 to 55 per cent. It may be hoped that it will be possible in time to make similar additional comparisons between the USSR and Western Europe.[18]

forty-nine

In appraising Soviet socialism, however, I have referred thus far only to static efficiency. We have yet to consider the Soviet performance from the standpoint of the important twin of this standard, dynamic efficiency. I turn to this in the next lecture.                                        November 9, 1967

III. Further appraisal and prospects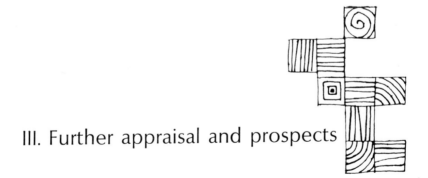

# III. Further appraisal and prospects

*Introduction*

I have distinguished between two kinds of efficiency in terms of which economic performance is appraised: static efficiency, or the degree to which a community is able to exploit material opportunities that are open to it within the limits of available technological knowledge, and dynamic efficiency, which relates to the community's capacity to add to its technological knowledge and to exploit such knowledge with increasing effect.

The two types of efficiency evidently are interrelated. Thus, static efficiency bears the imprint of dynamic efficiency of previous periods, while dynamic efficiency is a composite of advances over time in technological knowledge and in static efficiency. Yet each standard has an interest of its own. Both must be considered in any normative appraisal that pretends to completeness.

In examining Soviet economic performance I have referred thus far primarily to static efficiency. I turn now, therefore, to apply the standard of dynamic efficiency. As before, I focus on Soviet performance in utilizing available productive factors in different production units and in allocating them between production units.

*Differential trends in productivity and their causes*

Just as static efficiency affects the level of productivity, dynamic efficiency must affect its change over time. In trying to appraise dynamic efficiency, therefore, we may usefully refer to data that have been compiled on trends in productivity over time. These correspond to the data we considered previously on productivity levels.

Thus, national income or output per worker is now seen to grow at very different rates in different capitalist countries (Table 3). With a corresponding tempo of 4.7 per cent a year, the USSR, nevertheless, certainly performs well in comparison with these countries generally, but it is still matched or surpassed by several of them.

I have also extended similarly the calculations made previously of national income or output per unit of factor inputs, that is per unit of a composite of labor and capital taken together. This yardstick is related to that of output per worker in much the same way regarding changes over time as it was regarding levels at one time. Thus output per worker may grow at different rates not because of any differences in dynamic efficiency but simply because of differences in the growth of the capital stock with which labor may cooperate. By calculating the change in output per unit of factor inputs, we in effect allow for such variations in the growth of capital stock.

Table 3

Real National Income per Employed Worker and per Unit of Factor Inputs, Average Annual Rate of Growth, 1950-62, Selected Countries[a]
(per cent)

|  | National income per employed worker (1) | National income per unit of factor (labor and reproducible capital) inputs (2) |
| --- | --- | --- |
| United States | 2.4 | 2.0 |
| Northwest Europe | 4.1 | 3.4 |
| France | 4.8 | 4.1 |
| Germany | 5.6 | 4.6 |
| United Kingdom | 1.9 | 1.4 |
| Italy | 5.3 | 4.7 |
| USSR | 4.7 | 2.8 |

[a] With employment adjusted for changes in hours, though not proportionately. For sources and methods, see the Appendix.

fifty-three

If we apply here this more meaningful yardstick, different capitalist countries evidently still perform differently (Table 3). As for the Soviet Union, I have already referred to the difference between that country and the capitalist West regarding the share of income saved. A corollary has been the notably high rate of growth of the Soviet capital stock. The Soviet capital stock has grown at a notably high rate even in relation to the labor force. Hence the additional capital equipment provided each worker has also been especially great.

Predictably, therefore, with the growth of output per unit of factor inputs as the yardstick, the Soviet performance is less impressive than it was previously. Thus, the Soviet tempo is now but 2.8 per cent a year. At this rate, the USSR still outpaces a few capitalist countries, but is now itself clearly outpaced by a number of capitalist countries which it formerly approached.[1]

Among different capitalist countries, the rate of increase in productivity is relatively low in the United States. This is so whether reference is to output per worker or output per unit of factor inputs. Rates of increase of both output per worker and output per unit of factor inputs vary widely even among countries of Northwest Europe, but in terms of either yardstick the tempos there generally tend to be higher than the corresponding one in the United States. The tempo of productivity increase, however measured, is especially high in Italy, indeed even higher than that on the average in Northwest Europe.

As we saw, capitalist countries also differ regarding the level of productivity, but here the United States ranks first, the countries of Northwest Europe next, and Italy last. This ranking holds for both output per worker and output per unit of factor inputs. Among capitalist countries, therefore, there is some tendency for rates of increase in productivity to vary inversely with corresponding levels. That is, tempos tend to be high where levels are low and tempos low where levels are high.

The tendency is not very pronounced, but so far as it prevails it seems of interest that the USSR only approaches Italy regarding the rate of increase of output per worker, and falls quite short of that country regarding the rate of increase of output per unit of factor inputs. As will be recalled, in terms of the level of productivity, however measured, the USSR was on a par with Italy, and was with that country at the bottom of our list. The USSR is also matched or surpassed by France and Germany regarding the growth of output per worker. It is clearly surpassed by both countries regarding the growth of output per unit of factor inputs. This is despite the fact that both France and Germany start from a higher initial level in terms of either of the two measurements of productivity.

What may be concluded as to Soviet dynamic efficiency? As before, our data are subject to error. This is especially true of those for the USSR. We certainly must not take very seriously differences between this country and others of a fraction of a percentage point.[2]

As before, too, productivity and efficiency are related but not the same thing. In trying to read from trends in the former to dynamic efficiency, therefore, we must again consider complexities. It will suffice to refer briefly to two outstanding ones. First, labor quality is here again a variable. What counts now, however, is its change over time rather than comparative level. During the period since 1950, one might suppose that the USSR would have benefited at least as much from increases in labor skill as Western capitalist countries, but this must be left to separate inquiry.

Second, chiefly under the famous "virgin lands" program, the USSR has experienced since 1950 a vast increase in agricultural land in use. While the land was often of inferior quality, output per unit of labor and capital should have benefited. So far as it did, the USSR would have an advantage at this point, for there was no corresponding increase in farm land in use among the Western capitalist countries considered.[3]

I conclude that with dynamic efficiency as the standard Soviet socialism does not compare unfavorably with Western capitalism generally. Such a comparison, however, is also in no way especially favorable to Soviet socialism. Moreover, it is a familiar fact underlined here that different capitalist countries perform differently in respect of dynamic efficiency. If our calculations are at all indicative, performance probably varies in some degree inversely with level of productivity.

The inverse relation is not marked, but if it indeed exists this would not be surprising. Thus, where productivity is low the stock of technological knowledge should often be relatively limited. There are opportunities to increase it relatively rapidly, therefore, by acquiring new knowledge, not only through domestic innovation, but through technological borrowing from abroad. Where the level of productivity is low, static efficiency also tends to be low, and opportunities to raise it should be the greater.

If it is in order to compare the Soviet performance regarding dynamic efficiency with that of Western capitalism generally, then, it seems more so to compare it with that of Italy. To repeat, the two countries are together at the bottom of the list in terms of the level of productivity. With the Italian performance as a standard, however, that of the USSR is unimpressive. According to our calculations, dynamic efficiency in the USSR probably has not been as high as in Italy. Regarding dynamic efficiency, several countries of Northwest Europe, including France and Germany, probably also outmatch the USSR. This is despite the fact that the USSR starts from a lower level of productivity than these countries do.[4]

### The question of the period

I have been referring to the comparative Soviet performance during years since 1950. These are recent years following the most radical post-war adjustments. As such, they represent a particularly interesting period to consider. Nevertheless, is it not true that Western capitalist countries since the war have tended to perform well by their own historical standards? Even granting that another great depression is not in prospect, is it not likely that the current performance often reflects transient rather than persistent forces? What particularly of the possibility that one or another country even after 1950 was still "catching up" on opportunities left unexploited in the tumultuous war and immediate post-war years, and so was able to perform especially well on this account?

Available data on longer term trends in productivity in Western capitalist countries still leave much to be desired, but tempos of increase no doubt have often been higher since 1950 than over longer periods, whether early or recent. If post-1950 performance is to be considered in the perspective of longer-term trends in the case of capitalist countries, however, this is also in order in the case of the Soviet Union. Regrettably, for that country any lengthy historical period turns out to be notably turbulent. As a result, long-term trends in productivity are difficult to measure and difficult to interpret. Most likely, however, for the USSR, too, performance since 1950 has been relatively good by historical standards.[5]

On the questions posed, however, it is perhaps more illuminating to consider that in several, though not all Western capitalist countries, the most recent performance has not been quite so impressive as that of the early fifties. This is clearly so regarding growth of output per worker (Table 4). It may well be so also regarding growth of output per unit of factor inputs, and dynamic efficiency. The rate of growth of output per worker, however, has also declined in the Soviet Union. If we may judge from this yardstick, in the most recent years Soviet performance compares no more favorably with that in the West than it did for the early fifties.

These few facts hardly dispose of the thorny questions at issue. In the last analysis probably only the passage of time will provide us with any very satisfactory answers. For the present, however, it does not seem amiss to focus, as I have been doing, on comparative performance during the years since 1950.

*Innovation*

If Soviet performance regarding dynamic efficiency has been

fifty-seven

undistinguished, what is the explanation? The diverse forces affecting a country's dynamic efficiency almost defy summary appraisal. A cardinal aspect, however, is innovation, the acquisition and application of new technological knowledge. Efficiency regarding innovation is itself a rather involved matter,[6] but the relevant working arrangements under Western

Table 4

Real National Income per Employed Worker, Average Annual Rate of Growth, 1950-64, Selected Countries[a]

(per cent)

| | 1950-62 (1) | 1950-64 (2) | 1950-55 (3) | 1955-64 (4) |
|---|---|---|---|---|
| United States | 2.1 | 2.2 | 2.7 | 2.0 |
| Northwest Europe | 3.8 | 3.9 | 4.5 | 3.6 |
| France | 4.8 | 4.7 | 4.7 | 4.7 |
| Germany | 5.2 | 5.3 | 7.1 | 4.3 |
| United Kingdom | 1.6 | 2.0 | 1.4 | 2.3 |
| Italy | 5.4 | 5.2 | 5.3 | 5.4 |
| USSR | 4.5 | 4.3 | 5.5 | 3.7 |

[a] Employment *not* adjusted for changes in hours. For sources and methods, see the Appendix.

capitalism are obviously not always as might be wished. Most importantly, dissemination and use of new technologies are impeded by patents and commercial secrecy. No matter how effective patents and commercial secrecy are in encouraging innovation, the fact remains that from the standpoint of the community, once a new technology has been discovered and developed it is economic for it to be used as widely as possible. As the primers teach, the further use of available knowledge in itself entails no further cost. Restrictions on such use, therefore, whether through denial of or even the levying of a charge for access, are necessarily uneconomical.

As is still not always understood, however, the working arrangements affecting innovation under Soviet socialism also have their limitations. Restrictions on access to new technologies, whether through patents or otherwise, nevertheless are not one of them.[7] Inventors are rewarded for their achievements in the USSR, but new technologies are made available freely and without charge to all who might wish to use them. Government agencies, which avidly follow technological developments abroad, also circulate among interested parties the information they compile.

How useful such free access is, however, must depend on the interest of potential users to seek the new technologies out and apply them, adapting them to their own needs, where necessary. It is here that the Soviet working arrangements are faulty.

I have referred already to the aberrations of Soviet enterprise management. To the already long list of such oddities, we must add still another: a disinclination to change technologies. This, too, is a subject of continuing complaint in the USSR. The complaints sometimes are also illuminating as to the causes of managerial conservatism:[8]

> The explanation is, first of all, that the introduction of new technology involves certain risks and requires a considerable expenditure of time; secondly, after new technology has been introduced, more difficult plan targets are set and consequently there is less opportunity for fulfilling them and receiving bonuses.

For these reasons, managers are reluctant to innovate generally, but in the case of new products there is a further difficulty. The ruble prices adopted for them may prove to be relatively inadequate. For some time there have been, it is true, special rewards for introduction of new production processes and new products by management, but these apparently are very often too limited to serve as an inducement to such activities.

Under Soviet centralist planning, changes in technology if at all consequential must be undertaken on the initiative, or at least with the approval, of superior agencies. Here the attitude towards innovation is no doubt more favorable than in the enterprise. Indeed, superior agencies must be primarily responsible for the technological progress that has been realized.

Yet the organizations in question constitute a highly complex administrative structure. Some 400 research and design institutes serve the needs of machinery industries alone. More than a dozen agencies may have to be consulted about the design of a single product. Not surprisingly the enterprise manager who might otherwise have been inclined to propose a change in his technology is sometimes discouraged simply by the red tape involved. Whether because of the red tape or for other reasons, the superior agencies for their part may also be slow to take the initiative.

They may also be slow in completing their task, so much so that, according to a first deputy minister in machinery construction, "many examples" may be cited where the article produced becomes obsolete even before it appears: as with the new model of the "Zaporozhets" automobile, which has recently appeared six years after its inception but then could not compete with light automobiles produced in Italy and Western Germany as early as 1961-63.[9]

Even Krushchev once had occasion to concern himself with this phenomenon. It may be comforting to some in this city to learn that one of his complaints concerned the "intolerable slowness," due chiefly to "lack of coordination of design work," with which the oxygen-converter method of steel production was being introduced. Whatever the reason, Krushchev was right about the delays. As of 1962, the Russians were producing an even smaller share of their steel than the United States by use of the oxygen converter method.[10]

As Krushchev's famous further remarks on Gosplan officials in "steel blinkers" remind us, the failure of superior agencies to exercise initiative may affect not only introduction of a particular product or process, but choices between major technologies.

Where superior agencies have been lacking in initiative, as these examples suggest, the reasons are often found in familiar ailments of bureaucracy. But here, as elsewhere in Soviet planning, the limited development of economics must also be a factor. For example, obsolescence for long was apparently considered a phenomenon peculiar to capitalism. Hence it need not be taken into account in determining the retirement of old machinery and equipment.[11]

We must see in the light of these circumstances an outstanding feature of the Soviet technological scene: the extraordinary long-runs which are made for different products, including machinery. While such runs may sometimes be economical, they can easily be carried to excess. This must often be so in the USSR.

I have been focusing especially on the application of new technology. What of its origination? Among industrial engineers it is a truism that the line between these two activities is rather blurred. To apply a novel development, if it is at all basic, usually entails further work of a more or less novel sort, and this is the more true if the discovery is to be adapted to uses other than the one originally intended.

While reference has been to application, therefore, what has been said also relates to origination. But, to turn more expressly to the latter, I have already referred to the heavy reliance of the USSR on technologies developed abroad. Such technological borrowing was especially great during the early five year plans, but it apparently continues.

In the USSR, it is claimed, nevertheless, that the Russians have for long been developing new technologies at a notable rate. In 1960, some 10.5 thousand innovations were deemed sufficiently significant to be attested as inventions there. Several million additional developments were accorded the lesser status of usable rationalization measures.[12] Yet really consequential innovations of Soviet origin seem only rarely to be reported, either by the Russians themselves or by foreign observers. Authorities in this field appear to be of the view that, overall, the number of such basic innovations in the USSR has been quite limited compared with that in such countries as the United States, Germany, or England.[13]

Given its initial backwardness and the continuing opportunities to borrow knowledge from abroad, the USSR, of course, could not be expected to be highly original technologically. If here too, however, the Soviet working arrangements have sometimes been an adverse factor, this would not be very surprising.

Thus, in the USSR it is said that technological creativity is a mass phenomenon. In fact, at least in the case of rationalization measures, this must be a partial truth. But under centralist planning it cannot be easy for the independent inventor to obtain facilities and materials for an ambitious project, or to arrange for application of its fruits. Of this, the excruciating experiences of Lopatkin, the inventor hero of Dudintsev's *Not by Bread Alone*,[14] are surely a vivid testimonial. Moreover, while there are rewards for useful discoveries, these are rather limited: in 1960, for the author of an invention, typically less than 2,500 rubles, and for the author of a rationalization proposal, probably little more than 28 rubles. These are lump-sum payments.[15]

For purposes of promoting development of new technologies, then, the government must rely very largely on institutional research. In an economy that is at all modern, such research is said to have its merits, and no doubt it does. But in the USSR the agencies chiefly in question are the specialized ones already referred to. These apparently have the same bureaucratic failings in discovery of technologies as in their application. One wonders, therefore, how effectively the potential advantages of institutional research are exploited, and whether in any event technological creativity has not suffered because of the extreme concentration on institutional research at the expense of that of the independent inventor.

Under the five year plans, the government of the USSR by all accounts has brought about a radical transformation in industrial technology there. In doing so, however, the government, to repeat, has drawn heavily on foreign technologies.

To a greater degree than is often assumed, the transformation may also have been achieved under the early plans when the economy was advancing from initial backwardness. In any event, to return to the question posed earlier, in view of the working arrangements that have been described, the comparatively undistinguished recent Soviet performance regarding dynamic efficiency does not seem altogether surprising.

Dynamic efficiency, however, turns not only on technological innovation, but on changes in working arrangements that may improve a country's economic performance generally in the course of time. Such changes could be the subject of a separate discourse. Time permits me only to record that Stalin died on March 5, 1953. After that, in the period covered by our productivity data, the dictator's successors certainly sought to improve Soviet economic performance through changes in working arrangements. Indeed, they initiated notably many measures to this end. It would be surprising if some of these measures were not to the good. But it is not especially controversial, I think, to hold that, on balance, they must often have been otherwise. One may hold so even if he does not consider a principal architect of the new measures, Krushchev, to be as "harebrained" as his successors have charged.[16]

Economic working arrangements, of course, have also been in flux in the capitalist west. The changes that have occurred during years of interest have rarely been as numerous or as dramatic as those taking place in the USSR, but they could well have been more beneficent. After all, with all of their foibles, governments in many Western capitalist countries are surely conducting their economic affairs with increasing skill. Techniques and facilities for decision-making have also been improving in familiar ways in the private sector, and these developments too should have been favorable to efficiency. At any rate, here too there seems to be no reason to doubt our main finding regarding Soviet dynamic efficiency.

*Industrialization and efficiency*

I have been attempting in these lectures to gauge the economic merit of Soviet socialism, with efficiency as the standard of such merit. This is an elusive theme, but perhaps we have gained some insight into it. Thus, according to our inquiry, Soviet socialism, because of diverse shortcomings, is quite unimpressive in respect of static efficiency. By this standard, it may be comparable to Western capitalism, but only where that system is not functioning very well. In terms of dynamic efficiency, Soviet socialism is more or less a match for Western capitalism generally, but in the West, dynamic efficiency seems very broadly to vary inversely with the level of productivity. It is of interest, therefore, that in terms of dynamic efficiency the USSR seems to be outmatched by a number of Western capitalist countries which are on a par with or surpass it in terms of the level of productivity.

But some of my listeners may have wished long since to demur at these findings. In whatever way dynamic efficiency is related to the level of productivity, it should be related similarly to static efficiency. But must not static efficiency itself depend on a more basic aspect, the stage of economic development? Indeed, so far as there are differences in static efficiency among Western capitalist countries, must not differences in the stage of economic development be a principal cause? And where Soviet socialism is less efficient than Western capitalism, is this not due more often to the less advanced stage of Soviet economic development than to the socialist working arrangements employed? Is not Soviet inefficiency, in other words, more a phenomenon of relative economic backwardness than of socialism?

As usually understood, a country's stage of economic development turns on diverse aspects, but chiefly on the degree of industrialization. If we may judge from available but often defective data on this matter (Table 5), all of the Western capitalist countries covered are relatively advanced economically. By now, so also is the USSR. But some capitalist countries are more advanced than others, and the USSR is indeed to be compared with the less rather than more advanced capitalist countries.

## Table 5

### Indicators of Degree of Industrialization, Selected Countries, 1960[a]

| | Share of gross product originating in non-farm sectors[b] (per cent) (1) | Share of employment in non-farm sectors[c] (per cent) (2) |
|---|---|---|
| United States | 96 | 92 |
| France | 90 | 78 |
| Germany | 94 | 86 |
| United Kingdom | 96 | 96 |
| Italy | 83 | 68 |
| USSR | 71-80 | 58 |

[a] For the USA and Western Europe, see Denison, *Why Growth Rates Differ,* p. 206; OECD, *Statistics of National Accounts, 1950-1961,* Paris, 1964, pp. 27-28. For the USSR, see Stanley H. Cohn, *Derivation of 1959 Value Added Weights for Originating Sectors of Soviet Gross National Product* (Processed), Research Analysis Corporation, April 1966, p. 20; and the present study, p. 80, n. 18, and the Appendix.

[b] For all capitalist countries other than France and Germany, gross domestic product at factor cost. For Germany and France gross domestic product at market price. For the USSR, reference is in principle to factor cost, but the two figures cited probably differ chiefly because of differences in valuation procedures employed. The lower one relates to 1959.

[c] For Western countries, data include part-time workers and vary in scope, especially regarding coverage of unpaid family workers. For the USSR reference is essentially to full-time equivalent.

Among capitalist countries, moreover, the difference in stage of development is no doubt a factor in observed differences in static efficiency. But it is hardly the only factor. Thus, the United States is little if at all more industrialized than most Northwest European countries, but it must be more efficient than all of them.

Perhaps our inquiry does indicate only that in terms of static efficiency Soviet socialism is performing much as Western capitalism does at a similar economic stage. If so, this is

sixty-five

still an interesting finding. Perhaps, however, the inquiry indicates also that, even at a similar stage, the Western capitalism with which Soviet socialism is to be compared is still not Western capitalism at its best.

But intriguing as this question is, it is, I believe, somewhat beside the point. After all, what we wish to know is not so much how Soviet static efficiency compares with that of Western capitalism at a comparable stage, but how Soviet static efficiency will evolve in the future. Here it is instructive to consider that the Soviet economy is still not at a highly advanced stage. So far as industrialization has brought gains in static efficiency under Western capitalism, the presumption is that it will do so also under Soviet socialism. But, as is rarely considered, the gains need not be of the same kind and magnitude.

Industrialization may affect static efficiency in diverse ways. It may suffice to refer to a few of these that seem especially outstanding here. They also illustrate why the impact of industrialization on static efficiency in the Soviet Union is likely to be rather special. Among capitalist countries a principal reason why static efficiency varies with the degree of industrialization is probably found in a familiar proposition in the economics of development: countries undergoing industrialization, at least for a protracted period, are apt to be markedly in disequilibrium regarding the allocation of labor between agriculture and industry. The labor force in agriculture initially may be inordinately large and labor productivity there inordinately low. But labor transfers to industry can occur only in the course of time, and meantime there is static inefficiency. As the transfers occur, however, relatively unproductive employment in agriculture declines and static efficiency tends to rise. Among the capitalist countries considered here, circumstances such as these must prevail especially in Italy. They may also still have been of some importance lately in France and Germany.

As for the USSR, here too static efficiency must suffer materially because of the inordinately large employment in agriculture. But the volume of such employment in any country depends not only on the level of development of industry, but also on the working arrangements regarding the choice of technology, or capital-labor ratio in industry. I have already referred to the Soviet procedures bearing on this aspect. They certainly leave something to be desired. Although the corresponding working arrangements in the West also have their faults, it would not be surprising if under the Soviet procedures losses in static efficiency from the initially large agricultural population were incongruously large. And in the future, Soviet gains in such efficiency from labor transfers occurring as industrialization proceeds may well prove incongruously small. With the increased use of an interest-like test to limit excessive substitution of capital for labor in industry, however, this is less likely than it was formerly.[17]

Among the sources of static inefficiency under Western capitalism, it is difficult to rate highly the complexity of the economy itself: the number of enterprises, the variety of products, and the like. As we have seen, however, this is a cardinal factor in static inefficiency under Soviet socialism. The complexity affects especially the functioning of superior agencies; these have the onerous task of coordinating and directing economic affairs everywhere. Moreover, as a result of industrialization to date, the complexity is already notably great. There are now in the USSR 200,000 enterprises of "census size." According to a so-called "complete classification," these produce some 20 million distinct products.[18] As industrialization proceeds, the complexity will become still greater. Here then is an aspect of industrialization which affects relatively little static efficiency under Western capitalism, but can only be expected to impair such efficiency increasingly under Soviet socialism.

I have referred already to the beneficent change that has occurring lately in the attitude of the Soviet system's directors towards the consumer, their increasing concern to limit further exploitation of consumers in the interests of capital formation and growth. This change in attitude must reflect many factors.

sixty-seven

It does not seem far-fetched, however, to think that the progress of industrialization, with its concomitant gains in total output and consumer expectations, is among them. There may thus be still further ways rather peculiar to Soviet socialism in which industrialization must be affecting static efficiency. Here, however, the consequences are rather diverse.

On the one hand, with growth financed so largely as it was hitherto at the expense of consumption, there necessarily has been an adverse effect on incentives, and hence on static efficiency. We saw previously how this has occurred. Should consumers now be allowed to share more fully in the fruits of progress, therefore, incentives and static efficiency should benefit.

On the other, the task of superior agencies in coordinating and directing the economy must by the same token become the more formidable. The government formerly sought above all simply "to produce steel and then more steel." In effect it is now becoming much committed also to the more intricate imperative of satisfying increasingly the wants of millions of consumers; consumers, be it noted, who as they become more affluent are also becoming more choosey. Here then is another way in which further industrialization will tend to impair rather than enhance Soviet static efficiency.

Changes in static efficiency are, to repeat, an element in dynamic efficiency. And, while the foregoing trends are sometimes relatively novel, they all have already been operative in the Soviet Union in some degree. They must have affected Soviet dynamic efficiency in the past, therefore, along with other factors that I referred to earlier. There is still no basis, however, to feel that Soviet dynamic efficiency should have been other than undistinguished, as we concluded it was.

### Prospects further considered

But I have been tacitly assuming that in response to challenges and opportunities arising from industrialization, working arrangements themselves will remain unchanged. In appraising possible future trends in Soviet performance, must we not consider that, whether under the impact of industrialization or otherwise, working arrangements in fact have been evolving, and that they will continue to do so? Indeed, our inquiry into Soviet efficiency, both static and dynamic, has reached only up to the eve of the much-publicized economic reforms now in progress. Granting that the government's past measures to improve economic performance have not proven especially successful, are not the current measures much more promising?

What in any event of the recent progress in Soviet economics and its growing influence on planning practice, to which the current reforms testify? Does this not augur for significant economic gains, if not now, at least in the course of time? What particularly of the progress in mathematical branches? In alliance with associated developments in computer technology, will these not provide the Russians with the means to make centralist planning work? Alternatively, do not the current reforms already take the Russians toward a form of market socialism where there is wholesale decentralization and resort to market-like institutions? Is it not entirely possible, then, that the government, if it has not already done so, will in time commit itself fully to market socialism, with perhaps still more beneficent results?

The notion that Soviet performance might be much superior to what it has been in fact is not exactly novel. Rather it is one that proponents of socialism have been urging almost ever since the Bolsheviks came to power. It might be permissible to feel, therefore, that such a claim, even if true, could not be of great practical import. In any case, it is still very early to gauge the consequences of reforms that are still in progress. It is even earlier to gauge the consequences of possible reforms that may be still to come.

But in conclusion I should at least explain that the current economic reforms, while relatively novel, are not nearly so dramatic as many reports have suggested.[19] The government is manifestly decentralizing economic responsibilities. It is also adapting its principles of price formation and managerial success criteria so as to make them conform more nearly to the Western market pattern. Yet the rearrangements being made in both cases are only very partial. The reforms, thus, represent a step in the direction of market socialism, but only a very small one.

In the process of their being implemented, however, the reforms, it is true, have been evolving. Hence they may yet evolve still further. In any case, in trying to assess what our findings may portend for the future, one must certainly consider not only the current reforms but also that efficiency in the USSR has suffered hitherto from faulty economics, and that such economics is now on the mend. Indeed, Soviet economics has already progressed well beyond the doctrinaire and almost unbelievably dreary discipline that Stalin found it expedient to sponsor. The progress, it is true, has often been realized simply by mastery of branches of "bourgeois economics" that formerly were tabu. It is, however, nonetheless real on that account.

As suggested, contributors to the newer economic thought helped prepare the ground for the current reforms by their criticism of previous practice. I have drawn on this criticism in these lectures. The newer thought also helped shape the specific measures adopted. Hence it has begun to have an impact on practical affairs, practical affairs even of a kind which Stalin had expressly and jealously reserved for the Soviet "directing bodies," and so had proscribed for mere practitioners of the "political economy of socialism." These developments in Soviet economics are identified in the West chiefly with the name of E. Liberman, though it is only fair to say that many other Soviet economists have also contributed.[20]

In sum, forces making for rationality in economic thought and practice at long last have indeed been invigorated in the USSR. However much or little the current reforms achieve, such a trend in economic thought must ultimately be to the good. But how much so must depend on the evolving potentialities of the economics of socialism. These are certainly conjectural, but I trust no one will be shocked to hear that economics even at its best still has its limitations. This is also true of the economics of socialism. Writings in this field include some notable contributions, some composed as exchanges in the theoretic debate on socialist economic merit to which I have often referred.[21] But the design of economic working arrangements for a socialist society is still very much a fallible art rather than an exact science. Only the very committed will dispute this.

If Soviet economics was stunted under Stalin, furthermore, this was partly due to ideology.[22] It was partly due also to authoritarian politics. The dictator was sensitive to possible encroachments on his supreme power from any source, even the propagation and application of rational precepts which might limit arbitrary action. Now that rationality has been allowed a larger role, it is difficult to imagine that it ever again will be so circumscribed as in the past. But ideology and authoritarian politics have still not ceased their intrusion into economic calculation. They are hardly certain soon to do so. This too must be considered in assessing the possible future contribution of Soviet economics to Soviet efficiency.

As economics has been advancing generally in the USSR, so have mathematical branches, such as input-output analysis and linear programming, that lend themselves to application by use of electronic computers. The government has also been promoting the development of computer technology. As reported, it has begun, with the aid of electronic computers, to apply the mathematical techniques in question, at least experimentally, in some types of planning.[23] This trend too can only be expected to continue, and must be to the good, especially for the overburdened superior agencies. The new techniques should often be effective in their sphere.

Even these advanced procedures, however, have their limitations. Rapidly as the procedures are evolving, they presumably will continue to do so. With the advent of the electronic computer, a system of "perfect computation" has become imaginable, but hardly a practicality. Claims to the contrary are often advanced, but rarely by anyone who has pondered seriously the question at issue.

As for market socialism, I myself have urged elsewhere that it might be economically advantageous for the Soviet Union to shift even now to this system.[24] But this seems to be one of the many issues in the economics of socialism that remain unsettled. In weighing it, we may refer not only to theory but to practice, for by all accounts market socialism has been approached, if not realized, in Yugoslavia. We still have much to learn, however, about this fascinating case. While the Yugoslav government has often claimed notable successes, evidence otherwise abounds, evidence such as this comment by a prominent Croatian official:[25]

> . . . if suddenly we were to permit such a conflict of forces which would lead to the elimination from our economy of all which according to its present capabilities could not exist, it is most likely that the depth of the disproportions which have been created up to this time would show up so forcefully that the question would arise whether we could stand by and let the process take its full course.

We must, I think, still defer any final judgment on market socialism.

Even if market socialism should be economically advantageous, of course, the system's directors in the USSR could be expected to turn to it only if ideology should have eroded still further there, for they would have to accept wholeheartedly market processes which they had been bred as Marxists to consider anarchic. The government would also have to accept the further threat to its authoritarian power and to the bureaucratic status of superior personnel generally that would be inherent in an economic reorganization such as would be required, including the wholesale decentralization of decision-making. Such ideological and political preconditions for market socialism nevertheless may possibly materialize, so this system is not precluded.[26]

I have been referring primarily to the Soviet non-farm sector. It should be observed, therefore, that the government has lately by no means ignored agriculture, that measures being taken there, in the view of many Western authorities, are promising, that in the past the gap between promise and performance has nowhere been larger than in agriculture, and that in future this sector will no doubt continue to claim the government's attention.[27]

In pondering what the future may hold for Soviet efficiency, we must consider all these trends. Since we are interested finally in comparative efficiency, we must also consider that in Western capitalist countries efficiency, at least of the static sort, has tended lately to increase. Most likely it will continue to do so.

Marx held long ago that socialism must prove economically superior to capitalism. His followers ever since have reiterated this claim. Critics of socialism, however, have often sought to rebut it. We have examined the economic performance of this system in the USSR, where the fiftieth anniversary of its introduction is being celebrated. If we may judge from the Soviet experience, socialism has performed better than some critics have assumed, but hardly in accord with Marx's claim. Conjectural as the future may be, one is led to wonder whether this claim will ever be validated.

The two systems, to repeat, have evolved in the course of time and are certainly not quite so dissimilar as the alternatives Marx depicted. In future they may converge still more. But so far as the convergence stems from the economic imperatives that Marx himself stressed, socialism as found in the USSR should have to evolve no less than its rival in the West.

November 16, 1967

# Notes

In cross references from one note to another, the first number indicates the lecture referred to and the second the number of the note.

*Notes to Lecture I*

1. On the analytic discussion of socialist economic merit, see Abram Bergson, *Essays in Normative Economics*, Cambridge, Mass., 1966, Ch. 9; Abram Bergson, "Market Socialism Revisited," *Journal of Political Economy*, October 1967.

2. Austria may be an exception to the stated rule. Public ownership is very extensive there, though often of an indirect sort, while the political process is clearly not authoritarian.

3. See below, 1-7.

4. See Abram Bergson, *The Economics of Soviet Planning*, New Haven, 1964, Ch. 13, and Simon Kuznets, "A Comparative Appraisal," in Abram Bergson and Simon Kuznets, eds., *Economic Trends in the Soviet Union*, Cambridge, Mass., 1963.

5. In more technical terms, how much a community should save must turn ultimately on the pertinent values or preferences, preferences, that is, as to the division of the community's output between, on the one hand, current consumption, and, on the other, savings and hence growth, which might permit, though it does not assure, an increase in consumption in the future. Under capitalism, so far as savings are determined by the market the operative preferences are in effect those of households or their agents. Such "consumers' sovereignty" nevertheless has its critics, and regarding savings probably more than in other spheres.

But what is in question is the view to be taken of working arrangements of a sort which in the USSR have permitted the system's directors to determine savings instead in accord with their own preferences. Moreover, such so-called planners' preferences, as it has turned out, differ radically from those of consumers. What has been suggested is that in the West, even among those who are critical of consumers' sovereignty, few will deem this a virtue of the Soviet system. In less developed countries attachment to consumers' sovereignty no doubt is weaker than in the West, but even here responsible appraisal of Soviet-type working arrangements will be concerned with their efficiency as well as the capacity they confer to supplant consumers' by planners' preferences. At the same time, in the USSR itself planners' preferences regarding savings seem no longer to differ as much as they used to from those of consumers.

We are concerned with the share of a community's income that is properly saved. In economic analysis, this itself is often treated as an aspect of efficiency, but as implied I prefer to treat it otherwise. For present purposes, the question of the share of income saved seems best viewed, as it sometimes is, as bearing on equity, though inter-temporal equity rather than the intra-temporal equity already mentioned. Hence efficiency is understood not to embrace this matter.

6. See Bergson, *The Economics of Soviet Planning*, Ch. 6 and p. 328 and the sources cited therein; Lloyd G. Reynolds and Cynthia H. Taft, *The Evolution of Wage Structure*, New Haven, 1956, pp. 352ff; Simon Kuznets, *Modern Economic Growth*, New Haven, Connecticut, 1966, pp. 195ff.

7. To return to the two types of efficiency, within limits of available technological knowledge, one of the economic opportunities open to the community is that of acquiring more technological knowledge. For this reason, if the two types of efficiency are not to overlap, the static variety must be envisaged as referring to the functioning of working arrangements in spheres other than the production of new technological knowledge. This perhaps is also the usage most convenient here, though as is usually the case in empirical inquiry I cannot be very attentive to such a precise analytic distinction.

As theory teaches, an economy may perform more or less well over time depending in part on the degree of conformity to certain optimal principles concerning the sequence of mixes of goods that are used to reproduce themselves. Moreover, different economies may perform differently in this respect quite apart from any differences in the advances in technological knowledge. A difference in degree of conformity to optimal principles concerning the sequence of product mixes is not readily construed either in terms of the variation over time in the effectiveness with which available technological knowledge is exploited. Even so, however, performance regarding the sequence of mixes should properly be considered a factor in dynamic efficiency, but the evidence on dynamic efficiency to be considered seemed to bear primarily on aspects other than performance regarding the sequence of mixes. On dynamic efficiency, see p. 52, also below, 3-6.

8. The nature of the difference in results that emerges, depending on whether foreign, national, or U.S. prices are used, is also as would be expected. See, for example, Morris Bornstein, "National Income and Product," in Joint Economic Committee, Congress of the United States, *Comparisons of the United States and Soviet Economies*, Part II, Washington, 1959, pp. 386-387.

9. The foregoing characterization is most appropriate where inputs are aggregated "arithmetically." In fact, I aggregate inputs here by the alternative "geometric" procedure, which seems theoretically more defensible.

10. Denison first elaborated his method of adjusting for differences in labor quality in his *The Sources of Economic Growth in the United States*, New York, 1962. He explains it again in his *Why Growth Rates Differ*, Washington, D.C., 1967, on which I have drawn extensively in these lectures in compiling comparative data on Western capitalist countries. Although I have found it convenient to calculate output per unit of factor inputs according to a somewhat different procedure from that used by Denison, his work often sheds further light on the role of the diverse causes of differences in productivity among capitalist countries that have been observed.

11. Dollar earnings differentials in any event should serve as a basis for discounting female labor only in calculations in terms of dollar prices. In each of the alternative calculations in terms of foreign national prices, reference should be to corresponding foreign national earnings differentials. Data on this aspect, however, are not at hand. In the case of ruble prices, one wonders whether the male-female differential could be as large as that in terms of dollar prices.

12. See President's Committee to Appraise Employment and Unemployment Statistics, *Measuring Employment and Unemployment*, Washington, D. C., 1962, p. 220.

13. On the effect of the inclusion of land on calculations such as are made here of comparative factor productivity in the USSR and USA, see Bergson, *The Economics of Soviet Planning*, pp. 348, 363ff. As is evident from the data on factor shares in Denison, *Why Growth Rates Differ*, p. 38, inclusion of land could only have a negligible effect on calculations of the comparative factor productivity in Western Europe and the USA.

14. So far as technologies are "embodied" in capital goods in use, moreover, differences in their availability should be reflected in the comparative data compiled on capital stocks. But these are

crude measures, and probably reflect only imperfectly differences in the economic worth of different capital goods.

15. I referred previously to the fact that the rate of savings which is desirable for a community depends on the preferences to which reference is made, particularly whether these are consumers' or planners'. This is also true regarding the question now at issue, the mix of consumers' goods that is optimal. Moreover, while I assume in the text that the preferences relevant to this mix are those of consumers, it is often suggested that the Soviet system's directors systematically substitute planners' for consumers' preferences even here. Even if they should, we would of course still be free to appraise Soviet economic performance from the standpoint of consumers' preferences, if we so desired, but while it is not difficult to find examples of substitutions such as are in question, the system's directors surely would be foolish to supplant consumers' by their own preferences generally, even if they were capable of doing so, which is doubtful. At any rate, the deficiencies in quality and assortment to which I shall refer later have manifestly been of concern to the government as well as to consumers, though one may wonder whether the government until recently has been as concerned as it should have been.

As will be evident, I shall also be evaluating Soviet performance in terms of consumers' preferences when I come in Lecture 2 to consider the question of labor effort. But again it is not easy to imagine any plausible planners' preferences such that a different standpoint on Soviet efficiency would be indicated. In order, however, for a change in preferences between income and effort that is favorable to effort to be viewed as conducive to efficiency, it is stipulated that the new preferences must in some deeper sense be more satisfying to the worker than the old. This stipulation is appropriate where the consumers' own "welfare" is the more ultimate end (as it is usually supposed to be in the West), but it is easy to believe that the system's directors would consider it a strange limitation.

The question of the relation of planners' and consumers' preferences as it bears on Soviet efficiency is discussed at a number of points in my The Economics of Soviet Planning. For further consideration of this matter reference may be made to this study.

Notes to Lecture II.

1. See James G. March and Herbert A. Simon, Organizations, New York, 1958, Ch. 3.

2. See above, 1-15.

3. See above, 1-6.

4. For the USSR, the cited figure represents a reduction in the share of industrial labor paid on a piece-work basis from a peak level reached in 1953: 77 per cent. See Bergson, *The Economics of Soviet Planning*, p. 110. On the use of piece work in the USA and Western Europe, see Leonard Kirsch, *Wage Administration and Structure in the USSR since 1956*, Ph.D. thesis, Harvard, April 1967, p. 216; Walter Galenson, *A Primer on Employment and Wages*, New York, 1966, p. 41; R. Marriott, *Incentive Payment Systems*, London, 1957, pp. 43ff; International Labor Office, *Labor Costs in European Industry*, Geneva, 1959, p. 64.

5. G. Mdivani, "Trevozhnie dni" (Ominous Days), *Teatr*, 1958, No. 12, quoted in David Berg, "The Cold War on the Literary Front," *Problems of Communism*, September-October, 1962, p. 36.

6. Karl Marx, *Critique of the Gotha Programme*, New York, International Publishers' Edition, n.d.

7. Bergson, *The Economics of Soviet Planning*, pp. 109-110; Kirsch, *Wage Administration and Structure in the USSR since 1956*, pp. 158ff.

8. *Ibid.*, pp. 93-94.

9. The turnover tax, I believe, should have had an adverse effect on labor effort even though the factor charges in question are those indicated by Soviet costing practice, which admittedly is theoretically dubious. On the latter theme, see Abram Bergson, *The Real National Income of Soviet Russia since 1928*, Cambridge, Mass., 1961, Chs. 3 and 8. On the turnover tax in 1960, see Abraham S. Becker, *Soviet National Income and Product, 1958-1962*, Part II, RAND RM-4881-PR, May 1966, p. 125. See also below, 2-17. On the theoretic relation of taxes, labor effort and efficiency, see Bergson, *Essays in Normative Economics*, pp. 186ff.

10. See Bergson, *The Economics of Soviet Planning*, pp. 72ff, 133ff, 150ff, 287ff; Joseph S. Berliner, *Factory and Manager in the USSR*, Cambridge, Mass., 1957; David Granick, *The Red Executive*, New York, 1960; Barry M. Richman, *Soviet Management*, Englewood Cliffs, N.J., 1965; *Soviet Studies: Information Supplement*, January 1967, p. 27; *Pravda*, April 26, 1966; Jeremy R. Azrael, *Managerial Power and Soviet Politics*, Cambridge, Mass., 1966; Barry M. Richman, *Managerial Development and Education in the Soviet Union*, East Lansing, Michigan, 1967; *Pravda*, July 27. 1967.

11. See, for example, Galenson, *A Primer on Employment and Wages*, p. 58ff.

12. Emily Clark Brown, *Soviet Trade Unions and Labor Relations*, Cambridge, Mass., 1966.

13. Joseph Schumpeter, *Capitalism, Socialism and Democracy*, New York, 1947, pp. 212ff; P. J. D. Wiles, *The Political Economy of Communism*, Oxford, 1962, p. 257.

14. See, for example, A. Birman, in *Current Digest of the Soviet Press*, April 19, 1967, p. 15.

15. Bergson, *The Economics of Soviet Planning*, Ch. 8.

16. A Birman, in *Current Digest of the Soviet Press*, April 13, 1966, Part II, p. 3; Bergson, *The Economics of Soviet Planning*, Chs. 7, 11; Leon Smolinski, "The Scale of Soviet Industrial Establishments," *American Economic Review*, May 1962, No. 2; Leon Smolinski, "The Soviet Economy," *Survey*, April 1966; *Pravda*, October 13, 1965, and April 26, 1966.

17. As for the sources of inefficiency in collective farm agriculture, the ones most familiar in the West are the incentive-impairing government exactions and defective incentive arrangements generally. These are certainly important, but there are many others as well. It should be observed, however, that the government exactions have been a principal source of finance for industrialization. Here again, therefore, the government, in financing rapid growth, has had to pay a price in terms of efficiency. See Bergson, *The Economics of Soviet Planning*, Chs. 9 and 10.

18. For the comparison of the USSR and USA, reference is to the non-farm sector, excluding housing, and the output and inputs of labor services and capital employed in health care, education, government administration, and defense. Sources and methods are essentially as in the comparison of productivity for the economy generally. See the Appendix.

*Notes to Lecture III.*

1. The rate of growth of a country's capital stock actually depends both on the rate of investment and the initial stock relative to output, but as our data on factor productivity suggest the Soviet capital stock has in any event grown rapidly indeed: 9.3 per cent annually. Among the Western capitalist countries considered, the capital stock grows most rapidly in Germany, for which the rate of

increase is 6.4 per cent. For France the corresponding figure is 4.2. For Italy, curiously, it is only 3.5 per cent, which hardly differs from that of the United States, 3.6 per cent, or that of the United Kingdom, 3.4 per cent.

The cited figures all relate to reproducible capital, including fixed capital and inventories, but exclusive of housing and the capital stock of "general government." Indices of net and gross fixed capital are averaged, and the average index is then combined with one for inventories. See Appendix, Table 3.

2. For the USSR, an especially awkward aspect is the use of an arbitrary rate of return on capital as a basis to determine the share of this factor in the national income, and hence its weight in the aggregation of inputs that is made in the calculation of the rate of growth of factor productivity. This procedure was also employed in calculating the level of productivity in terms of ruble value weights, but there an alternative computation could properly be made in terms of U.S. price weights, and here ruble value weights are the only ones employed.

The rate of return used in both contexts, however, is 12 per cent, and it may be of interest that if alternatively a rate of return of 8 per cent is employed, the rate of growth of factor productivity rises from 2.8 to 3.3 per cent. Use of the 8 per cent return, however, would also mean that with ruble value weights the *level* of Soviet factor productivity is even lower than has been calculated.

With a rate of return of 12 per cent, labor receives a weight of 75 and capital a weight of 25 per cent in our calculations for the USSR. For Italy the corresponding figures are 80 and 20 per cent.

3. Denison, *Why Growth Rates Differ*, p. 181.

4. So far as there is a tendency among capitalist countries for dynamic efficiency to vary inversely with the level of productivity, it should be observed that this probably is something of a post-war phenomenon. Thus, I refer below to longer-term trends in productivity among capitalist countries. The available data for gauging these trends and their relation to productivity levels leave much to be desired, but as Professor Simon Kuznets has pointed out to me, it is difficult to discern even the limited relation that is observed in post-war years. As will also appear, however, the post-war economic performance of capitalist countries seems to differ from that over longer periods in regard to the degree of dynamic efficiency, and it does not seem excluded that a relationship to the level of

productivity that was previously obscure should now emerge more clearly.

In any event, the level of productivity is itself related to, but by no means wholly dependent on, the degree of industrialization, including the share of the labor force in agriculture. Moreover, at least for post-war years there can be little doubt that there as been some inverse relationship between dynamic efficiency and this aspect. Yet, a comparison of the USSR with Italy, and, though to a less extent, France and Germany, would be relatively apt from this standpoint as well as from the standpoint of productivity level. On the degree of industrialization and its relation to dynamic efficiency, see pp. 63-68, and Denison, *Why Growth Rates Differ*, Ch. 21. Denison should also be consulted on causes of differences among capitalist countries in productivity growth generally.

Although the USSR has been a borrower of technology (to turn to this matter), it should be observed that in the period in question it has been hampered by a factor that has little to do with efficiency: Western strategic controls. On the other hand, with its capital growing at an extraordinarily high rate, the USSR has had the opportunity to introduce rapidly the new technologies that have become available. So far as the government exploited this opportunity, therefore, the adverse impact of Western strategic controls on the growth of output per unit of factor inputs should have been at least partially offset.

5. Regarding longer-term trends in productivity, for the USSR a cardinal source of difficulty in measurement and interpretation stems from the notable relativity of measures of the growth of output in early years under the five year plans. Productivity grows relatively rapidly or very slowly in these years depending on whether output is calculated in "early" or in "late" ruble values.

This is not the place to pursue the methodological issue that is thus posed, but I should record that I have come to favor more than I did formerly the use of "late" prices in this context. This is partly because, as Professor Simon Kuznets has drawn to my attention, the "early" prices characterize not only an early stage of industrialization but one when the Soviet policy of economic isolation was already being implemented. In the circumstances, the "early" prices are likely to have been quite special. Also, in the case of available Western data on productivity growth, output often has been valued in relatively late prices.

On comparative long-term and post-war trends in productivity in the USSR and Western capitalist countries, see Bergson and Kuznets, eds., *Economic Trends in the Soviet Union*, especially the essays of Bergson and Kuznets; Richard Moorsteen and Raymond P. Powell, *The Soviet Capital Stock, 1928-62*, Homewood, Ill., 1966, Ch. 9; Angus Maddison, *Economic Growth in the West*, New York, 1964; and Simon Kuznets, *Postwar Economic Growth*, Cambridge, Mass., 1964.

6. It is involved even in theory. Among other things, it must be considered that imaginably a country could realize too much technological progress. Thus, the volume of resources devoted to innovational activity might conceivably be more than commensurate with the relative returns they yield. In fact, such a situation does not seem very likely, but even if it is excluded, appraisal of performance in this sphere must still consider that a country's returns to innovative activity may be relatively high not so much because it is especially creative as because it has many opportunities to borrow technology from abroad. I shall return later to this aspect.

7. On Soviet working arrangements for innovation, see Joseph Berliner, "Managerial incentives and decision-making," in Joint Economic Committee, Congress of the United States, *Comparisons of the United States and Soviet Economies*, Part I, Washington, D. C., 1959; Gregory Grossman, "Soviet Growth: Routine, Inertia and Pressure," *American Economic Review*, May 1960, No. 2; Alec Nove, *The Soviet Economy*, New York, 1961, pp. 151, 167-171; Khrushchev, in *Current Digest of the Soviet Press*, December 19, 1962; A. F. Garmashev, *Izobretatel'stvo i ratsionalizatsiia SSSR* (Invention and rationalization in the USSR), Moscow, 1962; Robert W. Campbell, *Accounting in Soviet Planning and Management*, Cambridge, Mass., 1963; Richman, *Soviet Management*, Ch. 9; Gregory Grossman, "Innovation and Information in the Soviet Economy," *American Economic Review*, May 1966, No. 2; E. Rakovskii, "Tekhnicheskii progress i faktor vremeni" (Technical progress and the time factor), *Planovoe khoziaistvo*, July 1966; *Current Digest of the Soviet Press*, September 27, 1967, pp. 3-6.

8. E. Manevich, quoted in Berliner in Joint Economic Committee, Congress of the United States, *Comparisons of the United States and Soviet Economies*, Part I, p. 364.

9. Rakovskii, *Planovoe khoziaistvo*, July 1966, pp. 15-16.

10. *Current Digest of the Soviet Press*, December 19, 1962, p. 4; Michael Boretsky, "Comparative Progress in Technology, Produc-

tivity and Economic Efficiency: USSR versus USA," in Joint Economic Committee, Congress of the United States, *New Directions in the Soviet Economy*, Part II-A, Washington, D.C., 1966, pp. 156-157.

11. Nove, *The Soviet Economy*, p. 151; Campbell, *Accounting in Soviet Planning and Management*, pp. 152ff.

12. Garmashev, *Izobretatel'stvo i ratsionalizatsiia v SSSR*, pp. 23-24.

13. See Institute of International Education, *Report of the IIE Seminar on Industrial Technology in the Soviet Union, March 24-25, 1960*, New York, September 1960, pp. 18ff; also Sir John Jewkes, "The Sources of Invention," *Lloyd's Bank Review*, January, 1958, pp. 19-23.

14. Vladimir Dudintsev, *Not by Bread Alone*, New York, 1957.

15. Garmashev, *Izobretatel'stvo i ratsionalizatsiia v SSSR*, pp. 194, 210ff.

16. The economic measures that the Soviet government has initiated since Stalin are by now the subject of a voluminous literature. It may suffice to refer here to Bergson, *The Economics of Soviet Planning*, and other writings cited therein.

17. On the pertinent Soviet working arrangements and their possible impact on the shift of labor from the farm to industry, see p. 47, and the sources cited in 2-16, especially Bergson, *The Economics of Soviet Planning*, Ch. 11.

18. Leon Smolinski, "The Soviet Economy," *Survey*, April 1966, pp. 90, 93.

19. See Gregory Grossman, "Economic Reforms: A Balance Sheet," *Problems of Communism*, November-December 1966; Alexander Balinky, Abram Bergson, John N. Hazard and Peter Wiles, *Planning and the Market in the USSR: The 1960's*, New Brunswick, New Jersey, 1967; Marshall Goldman, "Economic Revolution in the Soviet Union," *Foreign Affairs*, January, 1967; Keith Bush, "The Implementation of the Soviet Economic Reforms," *Radio Liberty Research*, March 8, 1967 (processed); Eugene Zaleski, *Planning Reforms in the Soviet Union, 1962-66*, Chapel Hill, North Carolina, 1967.

20. On the nature and practical impact of recent trends in Soviet economics, see the writings of Grossman, Balinky, *et al.*, and Goldman, cited above, 3-19; also I. V. Stalin, *Economic Problems of Socialism in the USSR*, International Publishers, New York, 1952; R. W. Campbell, "Marx, Kantorovich, and Novozhilov," *Slavic Review*, October, 1961; Marshall I. Goldman, "Economic Controversy

in the Soviet Union," *Foreign Affairs,* April 1963; Egon Neuberger, "Libermanism, Computopia, and Visible Hand: The Question of Informational Efficiency," *American Economic Review,* May 1966, No. 2; John Hardt *et al.,* eds. *Mathematics and Computers in Soviet Economic Planning,* New Haven, Conn., 1967.

21. See 1-1.

22. The term "ideology" is used variously. In these lectures, I have been using it in the sense explained in Peter Wiles, "Convergence: Possibility and Probability," in Balinky *et al., Planning and the Market in the USSR: The 1960's,* p. 98.

23. See above, 3-19, 3-20.

24. "Market Socialism Revisited," *Journal of Political Economy,* October 1967.

25. Dr. Vladimir Bakaric, leader of the League of Communists of Croatia, quoted in Egon Neuberger, "Central Planning and Its Legacies," in Alan Brown and Egon Neuberger, eds., *Foreign Trade of Centrally Planned Economies,* Berkeley, California (forthcoming). On the Yugoslav experience, see also *The Economist,* December 3, 1966, p. 21, and the sources cited in Bergson, *Journal of Political Economy,* October 1967, n. 20.

26. Compare Alexander Gerschenkron, *The Stability of Dictatorships,* Harvard Lecture, Yale University, April 3, 1963.

27. See Jerzy F. Karcz, "The New Soviet Agricultural Programme," *Soviet Studies,* October 1965; Alec Nove, "The Soviet Economy since Khrushchev," submitted at conference on *The Soviet Union after Khrushchev: Implications for Arms Control,* Nantucket, April 1967; *Current Digest of the Soviet Press,* May 3, 1967, June 8, 1967.

# Appendix

## The comparative data on productivity

Real National Income per Employed Worker and per Unit of Factor Inputs (Table 1): National Income per Employed Worker. For the comparative data for Western European countries and the United States, essentially I rely on Edward Denison, Why Growth Rates Differ. For national income (Appendix Table 1, cols. (1) and (2) ) reference is to net national product, at factor cost, output in each comparison between a Western European country and the United States being valued, on the one hand, in factor cost of the European country, and, on the other, in U.S. factor cost.

Northwest Europe includes all the European countries listed (except Italy) and, in addition, Belgium, Denmark, The Netherlands, and Norway. For the comparison of Northwest Europe with the USA, foreign national prices are apparently to be understood as representing average European factor cost. The comparative data on national income in Western European countries and the United States are from Denison, p. 22.

In comparisons between Western European countries and the USA, data on employment (Appendix Table 1, col. (5)) essentially reflect the methodology of the O.E.C.D., which means that initially they include part-time workers, and probably vary in scope to some extent as between countries. However, comparative employment data given by Denison, p. 51, are here adjusted to allow for differences in annual hours in conformity with indices of such differences given in Denison, p. 197. In compiling the latter indices, Denison discounts additional hours worked at varying rates, the rate used depending on the hours and the category of worker.

For the comparison of the USSR and the United States, I use preliminary results of a study of Soviet factor productivity that is in progress (to be referred to as Soviet Productivity) and which among other things involves a revision of calculations presented in my The Economics of Soviet Planning, p. 342, concerning the comparative levels of output and factor productivity in the two countries.

For national income (Appendix Table 2, row (a)), reference is to net national product, output in both the USSR and USA being valued, on the one hand, at ruble factor cost of 1955, and, on the other, at U.S. market prices of 1955. The calculations are broadly similar to those used in The Economics of Soviet Planning, but pre-

Appendix Table 1. Output and Factor Inputs, United States and Western Europe, 1960
(USA = 100 per cent)

| | Real national income | | Real national income, excluding income from housing and foreign assets | | | Employment | | Reproducible, non-government capital, excluding housing and foreign assets |
| | Based on foreign national price weights (1) | Based on U.S. price weights (2) | Based on foreign national price weights (3) | Based on U.S. price weights (4) | Adjusted for differences in hours (5) | Adjusted for differences in "quality" generally (6) | (7) |
|---|---|---|---|---|---|---|---|
| United States | 100.0 | 100.0 | 100.0 | 100.0 | 100.0 | 100.0 | 100.0 |
| Northwest Europe | 54.6 | 70.1 | 54.5 | 70.7 | 125.5 | 116.1 | 58.0 |
| France | 13.0 | 16.7 | 13.0 | 16.9 | 30.1 | 27.8 | 14.3 |
| Germany | 17.2 | 22.3 | 17.3 | 22.7 | 40.4 | 36.4 | 16.9 |
| United Kingdom | 16.5 | 21.0 | 16.3 | 20.9 | 37.5 | 35.3 | 16.2 |
| Italy | 7.1 | 11.9 | 7.2 | 12.2 | 32.2 | 27.1 | 9.6 |

viously I took as a point of departure comparative data compiled by Professor Morris Bornstein on the gross national product of the USSR and the United States in 1955. In the revision, I have recomputed the comparative levels of output of the two countries in 1955. Among other things, I have felt it in order to value farm income in kind at average realized farm prices rather than, as Bornstein does, essentially at retail prices, and to try to take account of additional information that has become available since Bornstein published his pioneer study.

Appendix Table 2. Output and Factor Inputs, USSR and USA, 1960

| Item | USSR (1) | USA (2) | USSR ÷ USA (per cent) (3) |
|---|---|---|---|
| a) Real national income | | | |
| In 1955 ruble factor cost, bil. | 1,185.0 | 3,419.0 | 34.7 |
| In 1955 dollars, bil. | 230.3 | 391.4 | 58.8 |
| b) Real national income, excluding housing | | | |
| In 1955 ruble factor cost, bil. | 1,191.4 | 3,446.8 | 34.6 |
| In 1955 dollars, bil. | 224.8 | 362.5 | 62.0 |
| c) Employment, mil. | 102.1 | 65.8 | 155.2 |
| d) Employment, in male, eighth grade equivalent, mil. | 81.2 | 66.9 | 121.4 |
| e) Reproducible capital, with selected omissions | | | |
| Fixed stocks, gross, in 1955 dollars, bil. | 331.0 | 691.6 | 47.9 |
| Fixed stocks, net in 1955 dollars, bil. | 237.4 | 386.4 | 61.4 |
| Fixed stocks, net and gross, average | | | 54.6 |
| Inventories, including livestock, in 1955 dollars, bil. | 125.5 | 123.3 | 101.8 |
| All | | | 63.9 |

For employment (Appendix Table 2, row (c)), reference is for the United States to persons engaged, in the U.S. Department of Commerce sense, which means full-time equivalent employment, and for the USSR to an aggregate which I believe is essentially comparable. For employment for the USSR, the principal changes from my earlier study reflect later information, particularly data in Nancy Nimitz, *Farm Employment in the Soviet Union, 1918-1962*, RAND RM 4623-PR, Santa Monica, November 1965. As in *The Economics of Soviet Planning*, no adjustment is made for differences between the USSR and USA in annual hours worked, since working time in the two countries seems very proximate.

*National Income per Unit of Factor Inputs.* For Western European countries and the U.S.A., comparative data on national income (Appendix Table 1, cols. (3) and (4) ), are essentially those used in the comparison of Western European and U.S. output per worker, but for present purposes I have adapted Denison's figures to omit income from dwellings and net income from foreign assets. The recalculation of comparative levels of national income that is indicated is determined from data on income from dwellings and foreign assets given by Denison, pp. 129, 132, and data on the shares of these items in national income in the USA and Western European countries in 1960-62, as given by Denison, p.38.

Employment is as in the comparison of output per worker. Reproducible capital (Appendix Table 1, col. (7) ) embraces structures, equipment, and inventories, including livestock. Stocks held by general government, however, are omitted, and so also is housing. For capital as so delimited, I use indices that Denison, p. 197, supplies of European stocks, relative to those of the U.S. Denison's indices relate to stocks per worker, but corresponding indices for stocks may be derived from his employment data on p. 51. For fixed capital, reference is to an average of an index of gross and an index of net stocks. While the Denison calculations reflect U.S. price weights, I use them in the calculation of factor productivity in terms of European price weights as well as in that of factor productivity in terms of U.S. price weights.

For each European country, in order to calculate aggregate inputs of labor and capital relatively to those of the USA, I weight the respective input indices by the corresponding factor shares in 1960-62, as given in Denison, p. 38. For the calculation of factor productivity in terms of U.S. prices, reference is to U.S. factor shares, while for the calculation of factor productivity in terms of European prices, reference is to factor shares in the European country in question. Inputs are aggregated by use of a geometric mean.

For the comparison of the USSR and USA, reference is again made to *Soviet Productivity*. National income (Appendix Table 2, row (b) ) is as in the comparison of Soviet and U.S. output per worker except that housing is omitted for both countries. As implied in Appendix Table 2, in terms of ruble factor cost, the net income, after depreciation, produced by housing, is negative in both the USSR and USA. Employment is as in the comparison of Soviet and U.S. output per worker. For reproducible capital (Appendix Table 2, row (e) ) reference for both countries is to structures, equipment and inventories, including livestock. For both, housing is omitted. For the U.S. I also omit government assets, and for the USSR the assets of broadly similar categories, e.g., health care, education, etc. For comparability with the Denison data used above, in the case of fixed capital reference is to an average of alternative index numbers of gross and net stocks in the two countries. Whether factor productivity is computed in terms of ruble or U.S. prices, reference for capital is to index numbers compiled in terms of U.S. prices. Underlying data on capital stocks that are employed represent a revision of those compiled in *The Economics of Soviet Planning*

In the calculation of factor productivity in terms of U.S. prices, inputs are aggregated with weights corresponding to U.S. factor shares for 1960-62, as given in Denison, p. 38. In the calculation in terms of ruble values, inputs are aggregated by use of these weights:

|  | Per cent |
|---|---|
| Employment | 75 |
| Reproducible capital | 25 |
| All | 100 |

These data correspond to synthetic ruble factor shares. For reproducible capital I impute a return of 12 per cent to net assets.

In both the computation in terms of U.S. prices and that in terms of ruble values, inputs are aggregated by use of the geometric mean.

*Real National Income per Employed Worker and per Unit of Factor Inputs, with Employment Adjusted (Table 2).* The national income data considered in the calculation of output per worker are as in Table 1, cols. (1) and (2). As for the employment data, for those relating Western European countries to the United States (Appendix Table 1, col. (6) ), I simply adjust here the employment data given

ninety-one

in Denison, p.51, by reference to "quality" coefficients compiled by Denison, p. 197.

Denison reduces the labor force of each country in question to its male, eighth grade equivalent by application of adjustment factors which are derived from differentials in earnings that prevail among U.S. male and female workers of different degrees of education. In compiling his overall coefficient of the quality of labor in any European country compared with that in the United States, Denison also allows in a similar way for broad differences in age structure. The quality coefficient that is used here also reflects differences in working time, as calculated by Denison.

In comparing employment in the Soviet Union and the United States (Appendix Table 2, row (d) ), I again use calculations in *Soviet Productivity*. For each country, I reduce employment to male, eighth grade equivalent by applying the adjustment factors for workers of different sex and degree of education that Denison derived from U.S. earnings differentials. I do not allow here for differences in age composition. To repeat, hours of work in the two countries appear to have been quite similar in 1960, so no adjustment was made for this aspect, either.

The calculations of output per unit of factor inputs are as in Table 1, cols. (3) and (4) except that the measures of employment used are those adjusted for quality explained above.

*The Rate of Growth of Output per Worker and per Unit of Factor Inputs (Tables 3 and 4).* In Table 3, for the United States and Western European countries, reference is to net national product, the output of each country being valued at constant factor cost of the countries concerned. For the data used (Appendix Table 3), see Denison, pp. 17, 192. Employment and capital stock indices (Appendix Table 3) are taken from Denison, p. 190. For employment, the data given by Denison are adjusted to allow for changes in hours, as indicated by him on p. 190. As with the indices of differences in hours mentioned above, those for changes in hours over time involve application of varying discounts, depending on the hours and the category of worker.

Employment and the capital stock have the same scope as in Table 1. In the case of fixed capital, reference as before is to averages of indices of gross and net stock, though here the data are in constant national prices of the country in question. For each country, inputs are aggregated geometrically by reference to national factor shares for 1960-62. See Denison, p. 38.

Appendix Table 3. Output and Factor Inputs, United States and Western Europe, Average Annual Rate of Growth, 1950-1962
(Per cent)

| | USA | Northwest Europe | France | Germany | United Kingdom | Italy |
|---|---|---|---|---|---|---|
| Real national income | 3.3 | 4.8 | 4.9 | 7.3 | 2.3 | 6.0 |
| Employment | 1.1 | .9 | .1 | 2.0 | .6 | .6 |
| Employment adjusted for changes in hours | .9 | .7 | .1 | 1.6 | .4 | .7 |
| Reproducible capital, non-government, excluding housing, foreign assets | 3.6 | 4.5 | 4.2 | 6.4 | 3.4 | 3.5 |

ninety-three

For the USSR (Appendix Table 4), I again draw on *Soviet Productivity*. For real national income, I refer to net national product in "adjusted rubles" of 1959. Here I take as a point of departure a series on the Soviet gross national product compiled in Stanley Cohn, "Soviet Growth Retardation," in Joint Economic Committee, Congress of the United States, *New Directions in the Soviet Economy*, Part II-A, Washington, D.C., 1966. In a letter to me of January 27, 1967, Cohn kindly elaborated on the summary data presented in this report. The Cohn series is here adjusted for depreciation.

Appendix Table 4. Output and Factor Inputs, USSR, Indices 1950-64
(1950 = 100 per cent)

|  | 1962 | 1964 |
|---|---|---|
| Real national income | 206.1 | 226.3 |
| Employment | 121.0 | 124.9 |
| Employment adjusted for changes in hours | 118.1 | 121.7 |
| Reproducible capital, excluding housing | | |
| Gross | 315.9 | n.a. |
| Net | 333.1 | n.a. |
| Gross and net, average | 324.5 | n.a. |
| Inventories | 264.6 | n.a. |
| Livestock | 159.2 | n.a. |

For the USSR employment is of the same scope as in Table 1. Reference is to non-residential capital stock, an average being taken of indices of gross and net stock in 1950 ruble prices. For employment, I revise and extend the series in Bergson, *The Real National Income of Soviet Russia*, pp. 442ff. I take into account here data in Nimitz, RAND RM 4623-PR; Joint Economic Committee, Congress of the United States, *Current Economic Indicators for the USSR*, Washington, D.C., 1965, pp. 63ff; and Murray Feshbach, "Manpower in the U.S.S.R.," Joint Economic Committee, Congress of the United States, *New Directions in the Soviet Economy*, Part III, Washington, D.C., 1966. I adjust for changes in hours in conformity with Denison's methodology, using data in Bergson, *The Real National Income of Soviet Russia since 1928*, pp. 425ff; in *The Economics of Soviet Planning*, and in the two handbooks of Tsentral 'noe statisticheskoe upravlenie, *Narodnoe khoziaistvo SSSR v 1960* (National Economy of the USSR in 1960), Moscow, 1961, p. 645, and *Narodnoe khoziaistvo SSSR v 1964* (National Economy of the USSR in 1964), Moscow, 1965, p. 590.

For data on the Soviet capital stock, I rely on Richard Moorsteen and Raymond P. Powell, *The Soviet Capital Stock, 1928-1962*, Homewood, Ill., 1966.

Inputs are aggregated geometrically by reference to the synthetic ruble factor shares already derived. Of the total weight assigned reproducible capital, 25.2 per cent, I allocate 16.2 per cent to fixed capital, 7.3 per cent to inventories, and 1.7 per cent to livestock.

In Table 4, real national income is as in Table 3, and so too is employment, except that no adjustment is made for changing hours. Sources and methods are also as before, but for the USA and Western European countries see Denison, p. 18. For the USSR, the data on output and employment used are shown in Appendix Table 4.